T0022560

Let's Talk About
PEER PRESSURE

Let's Talk About
PEER PRESSURE

By
Carolyn B. Anderson

E-BookTime, LLC
Montgomery, Alabama

Let's Talk About Peer Pressure

Copyright © 2007 by Carolyn B. Anderson

All rights reserved. No part of this book may be reproduced or transmitted in any form or by any means, electronic or mechanical, including photocopying, recording, or by any information storage and retrieval system, without permission in writing from the copyright owner.

ISBN: 978-1-59824-547-9

First Edition
Published June 2007
E-BookTime, LLC
6598 Pumpkin Road
Montgomery, AL 36108
www.e-booktime.com

Unless otherwise indicated, all Scripture quotations are from THE LIVING BIBLE, copyright © 1971. Used by permission of Tyndale House Publishers, Inc., Wheaton, Illinois 60189.

Scripture quotations marked from the Amplified translation are from THE AMPLIFIED BIBLE, Old Testament copyright © 1962, 1964, 1965, by the Zondervan Corporation. The Amplified New Testament copyright © 1954, 1958, by The Lockman Foundation. Used by permission.

Contents

Introduction

"David!"

"Yes, Father!" answered David. Hearing his father's voice loudly and clearly, he hurried to answer him. He knew his father wouldn't call his name unless he wanted him for something, so he rushed to see what he could do for his father.

"David, I want you to take these provisions to your brothers," his father told him.

David knew exactly where he was to go. David was the youngest son out of eight sons of Jesse, his father. His three older brothers, Eliab, Abinadab, and Shammah, had gone into battle for King Saul against the Philistines. Red-haired and fair-skinned David was taking care of the sheep for his father. Actually, he worked for King Saul, too, but he divided his duties between the king and his father. He was considered too young to go to battle.

David's father continued with his instructions, "When you take these provisions to your brothers, see how they are doing and come back and tell me how they are."

"Okay, Father," David answered obediently.

He quickly packed the provisions and made his way to the battleground site. As he drew near, he saw the Israelites gathered on one side and the Philistines on the opposite side. Leaving his packages with the person who was keeping the baggage, he ran into the midst of the Israelites to find his brothers. He was so excited to see them.

As they talked together, a loud deep voice bellowed from the ranks of the Philistines. "Hey!" the voice yelled, "What are you people doing fighting against us? Come on! Pick one man from the midst of you and let HIM come and fight with me. There's no point in all of you fighting. Just send that one. If he wins, we will serve you, but if I win, YOU will serve us. I defy the ranks of Israel this day."

David turned to look toward the sound of that belligerent voice. What he saw was a sight to behold for there before his eyes stood a man over nine feet tall, covered in armor and spouting defiant words against God. David could hardly believe his ears. Who was this fool who dared to speak against God?

The fool's name was Goliath and he was a giant. When he said that he defied the ranks of Israel, he was actually saying that **he defied the God of Israel.** He was saying that if he beat the Israelites that their God didn't have any power and wasn't worth serving. Those were fighting words.

Goliath just stood there clothed in his heavy armor. His coat of mail, which covered most of his upper body, weighed about 200 pounds. The tip of his spear, just the tip part, weighed 25 pounds. Armor covered his legs. In Goliath's own mind, he was unbeatable.

He wasn't unbeatable in David's mind, though. This mouthy arrogant Philistine had shouted against his (David's) God. David loved God with all his heart and did his best to follow Him. He loved God's Word. He loved to hear about God. He loved to play his harp for Him. He loved to sing to Him. How dare this heathen spout such garbage against HIS God!

He looked at the Israelites around him. All of them were cowering in fear. Every time they would run out to do battle, Goliath would lumber forth with his massive body and armor and start yelling. Their immediate reaction was to turn and run like a bunch of rats—IN THE OPPOSITE DIRECTION.

David heard some of the men talking, "The king has said that the man who kills that giant will receive great riches and will also receive his daughter AND his father's house will be tax free."

David heard them and questioned them about it. As he was doing that, his oldest brother, Eliab, heard him. Anger erupted in him at what David had said. He turned on David with a wrathful look and with an unkind voice said, "Why did you come here? You're supposed to be taking care of a FEW sheep. Who's taking care of those FEW sheep? Did you shirk your responsibility? I know what's in your heart. Your heart is evil and you presume things that you aren't going to get to do. You came down here just to see what is going on."

David looked at his brother wondering why he suddenly turned on him. "What did I do? I was just asking a question."

Then, he turned AWAY from his brother, Eliab, and turned to another person and asked the same question. He didn't allow his brother's words to deter him from his purpose for being there that day. His brother had called him a liar. David came to the battlefront because his father had told him to, but Eliab didn't bother to discover the truth. Out of his fear and anger, he turned on David to ease his own conscience and not look bad in his other brothers' sight, plus the sight of his fellow comrades.

King Saul found out that David was willing to fight Goliath so he sent for him. He insisted that David wear heavy armor, but David quickly realized that he couldn't maneuver in that. He was going against that heathen giant in the name of God and that armor wouldn't help him.

David went to a brook and chose five smooth stones. He put them in his shepherd's bag, took his sling, and went toward the Philistine. The Philistine jeered at David. He cursed him by his gods. Guess which "god" was going to win? This was the day that the Most High God was going to be heard.

David announced his intentions and gave Goliath fair warning. **"You come to me with a sword, a spear, and a javelin, but I come to you in the name of the Lord of hosts, the God of the ranks of Israel, Whom you have defied. This day the Lord will deliver you into my hand; and I will smite you, and cut off your head; and I will give the corpses of the army of the Philistines this day to the birds of the air and the wild beasts of the earth; that all the earth may know that there is a God in Israel." (I Samuel 17:45, 46 Amplified)**

What was David doing? He was stating that this incident was going on record. It was being written down and the result would be that God, the Most High God, would win. If you have read the story in I Samuel 17, then you know who won.

I want to go back to David's older brother, Eliab. Focus on his actions and his words. Would David have prevailed over Goliath if he had allowed his brother's words to hinder him? No. His brother was attempting to pull him aside and get him in a defensive mode. Do you know what I mean by that? Have you ever had friends who said things to you which you knew to be untrue, and really, you knew your friends knew to be untrue, but they said it just because they wanted to put you in a defensive mode. They wanted to MAKE you explain your actions. What is that? Pressure. They were pressuring you to do something that wasn't necessary to do.

When your parents hold you accountable and expect you to explain your actions about something, that's not the same. Your parents are in a position of authority in your life. They have been placed by God in that position so don't look at them in the same manner as your friends. Your friends are not authority figures in your life.

No matter how dear your friends are, you will have some over the years who will attempt to pressure you into doing or saying things you shouldn't. They may use anger to attempt to get you to do something they want or they may cry or use some other emotional hold to try to "force" you to yield to pressure. Notice that Eliab became angry. When? When Eliab heard David asking questions. What kind of questions was David asking? His questions were indirectly asking why they were sitting on this side of the battle not doing anything and not going forth in the name of the Lord. His questions made Eliab uncomfortable and caused them to look like the timid creatures they were. Actually, what David did was expose them for just what they were. Their inner selves were brought out for all to see. It wasn't pretty and Eliab wanted David to shut up.

What did David do in reaction to Eliab's questioning and statements? He really didn't react much. He said enough and then **turned his back** on Eliab. What was he indicating to Eliab's words? He was finished with them. He was through listening to them and he continued on his quest for the answers to his questions.

You are going to find out in this book about peer pressure, what its desire for you is and how you are supposed to react to it. You will find out that you must do as David did in this situation with his brother. You will have to turn your back on some things in order to not yield to peer pressure or be influenced by it. Go to chapter one and let's begin by learning just what peer pressure is.

Chapter 1
What is Peer Pressure?

Before we define the phrase "peer pressure," let's define the word "pressure." According to Webster's dictionary, here are a few of the meanings of this word: *"harassment; oppression; a constraining or compelling force or influence." (1)*

Now, can we make that definition a little simpler and more understandable? Yes!!! We can say that the word "pressure," used as someone pressuring you, means that this person is harassing or bothering you. It is a deliberate thought-out action that has a purpose. Maybe this person wants you to do something so he deliberately bothers you expecting a result. In this person's mind, he has an intended result, something he plans to see as a result of his persistently bothering you. This person may use words or threats to press against your mind to cause you to bow to what he wants you to do. He is ONLY concerned with what he wants, not what you want or need to do in the situation.

Think about a big wind coming against you. Have you ever been outside when it was extremely windy and the force of the wind was so strong that it almost knocked you down? That force from the wind coming against you or anything in its path is a PRESSURE against you. You can physically feel the wind coming against you and you have to STAND AGAINST IT or be swept away with it. If you allow yourself to be swept away with the wind, the wind will carry you to where IT wants you to go which isn't where you're supposed to be. That wind could sweep you off a cliff or sweep you in front of a car or just knock you down and cause you to skin your knee.

Pressure tries to make you conform or fit a situation that IT has designed for you. Now, when you add the word "peer" to that, you get the phrase, "peer pressure." Who are your peers? They are those people around you in your age group or your social group. As we said before, we aren't talking about authority figures such as your parents, your teachers, or others who are in those positions. These people aren't your peers. They have been placed in your life as authority figures and you are to obey them as such.

What is peer pressure? Peer pressure is a force that is used against you to cause you to conform to the wishes of someone of your own age or social group. In other words, it could be someone in your own grade or someone you play with after school who is trying to get you to do something that you don't want to do or you know is wrong to do. They are "pressuring" you by harassing you or trying to embarrass you because you won't do as they wish. They may even threaten you by saying they are going to tell something that you did or they might say they are going to do you bodily harm. Peer pressure is in the same category as bullying. God doesn't look at it any differently. It's a form of intimidation. It has its roots in fear. It's trying to cause YOU to fear and be afraid of what someone will do to you or what will happen to you.

Peer pressure tries to tell you that you don't have a place unless you yield to its force. Peer pressure says, "Hey, come join us so you'll fit in. If you don't join us and do what we do, then you're not a part of anything." **Peer pressure lies.** God has a place for you, and you will see from God's Word in a later chapter that you aren't supposed to "fit in" according to the way people say you are. You "fit in" the way God says.

Peer pressure is a yoke. Have you ever seen a yoke of oxen? A yoke is this heavy wooden thing that has an opening for two oxen necks. It is all one piece and cannot be separated. When people used oxen to pull a wagon or plow a field, they would put this yoke on them to keep the oxen together and keep them walking at the same pace.

If one ox decided to bolt and run, the other one had to go along because he was YOKED to that runaway ox. If the runaway ox decided to jump off a cliff or run into the water, the other ox didn't have any choice except to jump off the cliff or run into the water with the runaway one. It didn't matter that the sane ox didn't want to die or get wet; he didn't have any choice. He was YOKED to that insane ox.

Peer pressure has the same effect as those yoked oxen. If you YOKE yourself to it, you will be jerked around wherever your peers want to take you. The only thing is that you have the power to UNYOKE yourself from them. Jesus Christ died and rose again so you would have that power through His name. God gave you a will so you could CHOOSE if you wanted to be yoked to something like that.

What does Jesus say about yokes? Does He have anything to say? Of course. I wouldn't have asked the question if I didn't know the answer. I was just trying to get you to think about it. Matthew wrote Jesus' sayings about this in chapter 11 and verses 28 through 30.

"Come to me and I will give you rest—all of you who work so hard beneath a heavy yoke. Wear my yoke—for it fits perfectly—and let me teach you; for I am gentle and humble, and you shall find rest for your souls; for I give you only light burdens."

That was quoted from The Living Bible. Now, I want to quote verse 30 from The Amplified Translation of the Bible.

"For My yoke is wholesome (useful, good)—not harsh, hard, sharp or pressing, but comfortable, gracious and pleasant; and My burden is light and easy to be borne."

Did you notice what Jesus said about His yoke in relation to the word "pressure"? He said that His yoke was not pressing. His yoke doesn't pressure you to be something you're not supposed to be or pressure you to go somewhere you're not supposed to go. His yoke is good for you. His yoke is useful; it has purpose in your life. His yoke gives you purpose. When you yield to peer pressure, that takes away your purpose in life. When you yield to peer pressure, you have given someone else the authority to tell you what you're supposed to be doing and where you're supposed to be going. Actually, what you have done is made them your god, and we know what God said about having other gods before Him.

What are some other words that we can use to describe peer pressure drawing from Matthew 11:28-30? What your peers are pressuring you to do does not fit you. It is constantly **making you work to please** whoever is controlling the yoke. You may work and work to please him but you never will. Once you reach the point at which you think you have pleased this person, he will come up with another reason why you haven't and assign another hard task for you to do to "please" him. Peer pressure never lets you rest. You can never relax, for about the time you think you can, here comes another "pressure" which requires that you get up and do something else.

There isn't anything pleasant or gracious about peer pressure. It is always demanding your attention and, if you are yielding to it, you are always being "led around by the nose." You cease becoming an individual, and you become what the people exercising the peer pressure want you to become. THEY have set the course for YOUR life. Is that the way it's supposed to be? Do they have the last word where your life is concerned? Let's go to the next chapter and see.

ಐ ~ ೞ

Review Questions for Chapter 1

1. How would you define peer pressure?

2. Have you ever experienced peer pressure?

3. In what is peer pressure rooted?

4. Does peer pressure allow you to think for yourself? Why?

5. Give the Scripture reference in which Jesus talked about His yoke.

6. How does Jesus' yoke fit?

7. What does peer pressure do to you if you yield to it?

Chapter 2
You're "One of a Kind"

Have you ever heard the expression, "That's one of a kind," referring to a particular object? That phrase means that the object is special and there isn't another one just like it. Well, God created you as "one of a kind." You're special and there is not another person on this earth just like you. God created you with a unique personality, unique fingerprints, and everything about you unique because He created you to be YOU, not someone else.

Peer pressure is always trying to take that uniqueness AWAY from you. Peer pressure never adds to you or enhances or makes your life better. It is a thief and needs YOUR uniqueness to feed it. Why do you think that is? Why do you think peer pressure needs YOUR uniqueness? I know I ask a lot of questions but the purpose is to spur you to think before you read the next line.

- **Could it be that without your uniqueness, peer pressure doesn't have any power over you or anyone else?**
- **Could it be that peer pressure just isn't peer pressure without you?**
- **Could it be that peer pressure wants to hijack your uniqueness into its gang so that it will become a giant of power based on stealing what God created you to be?**

God created you to be YOU and you have to stand for what He created you to be. It takes determination and a willingness to allow others to fade from your life if necessary so that you can follow God's plan. Oops!!! I let it slip. . . .the secret's out. Did I say that God had a plan for you? Did those words just fly off the ends of my fingers and onto the keys of my computer? Now, really, did you think God would create you as a unique individual and not plan for that uniqueness? Come on now. You knew God was bigger than that. Yes, you did. Don't deny it. Way down deep inside your spirit man, you knew that God had a plan for your life. It was sort of a background knowing even though, possibly, no one had mentioned it to you. Let's look at God's Word on the subject. Here David is talking.

Psalm 139:13-16
"You made all the delicate, inner parts of my body, and knit them together in my mother's womb. Thank you for making me so wonderfully complex! It is amazing to think about. Your workmanship is marvelous—and how well I know it. You were there while I was being formed in utter seclusion!"

Now, here's where you need to really pay attention.

"You saw me before I was born and scheduled each day of my life before I began to breathe. Every day was recorded in your Book!"

Here is verse 16 from the Amplified translation.

"Your eyes saw my unformed substance, and in Your book all the days of my life were written, before ever they took shape, when as yet there was none of them."

Here are two BIG questions that you can answer from verse 16. I'm not giving you the answer. You read it for yourself and say the answers out loud.

- **When did God see you?**
- **When did He schedule each day of your life?**

All right, I'll give you a hint. The answer to both questions starts with the word "before."

Here's another question.

- **What did He record in His book?**

Let's talk about the word schedule for a moment. Every child who has attended school has had to follow a schedule. That schedule was set by someone else. In elementary school, the teacher sets the schedule as to when his students will have reading, math, science or other subjects. Usually, he spends so many minutes on a particular subject, then he will switch to another subject. Somewhere in the day, he has scheduled a few minutes for recess, and the principal has scheduled for the whole school to have lunch during a certain time. The school you attend has a schedule of when classes start and when classes end. When you are older and attending higher grades, you may be able to choose your own schedule to a point. That means you may choose which classes you wish to take, but you still have to follow a schedule. **It simply means that at a certain time, you are supposed to be at a certain place.**

God has a schedule made out for you, but it's not written down on paper where you can get the book and read it. The book exists, but it is in heaven where God has everything recorded that you are to become and how you are to get there. Yes, I would love to see my book and take notes, but that wouldn't be living by faith. God is a faith God and what we receive from Him, we have to use our faith to get it.

If you want to follow God's plan for your life, you're going to have to use your faith. What does that mean? That means that you're going to have to trust God. That means you're going to have to read His Word and learn about Him. That means you're going to have to spend time with Him in prayer. **That means you're going to have to become "God conscious" instead of "peer conscious." Your peers will never get you to where God has scheduled you to be in HIS book.** They don't have the power to do it. They can take you down and WAY off God's pathway, but they can't take you down God's pathway that has been designed just for you. They don't know what it is. Only God knows and YOU will only know as you walk with Him.

Will He reveal everything about your life in one fell swoop? No. What did I just say that God is? He is a God of what? . . . .what did I say? . . . .a God of FAITH, and how did I say that you would receive from Him? . . . .how? . . . .by using YOUR faith. Your faith connects with God's faith and pulls from Him what you need WHEN you need it. You don't need to know your WHOLE life at one time. It would probably scare you to the point that you would just back off and hide in a corner. You have to ask God daily for what you need for that day and what you're supposed to be doing that day. Now, He will reveal things about your future to you along and along, but you just store those things inside you and keep believing Him daily for His perfect will to be done in your life.

Allow God to separate you unto Himself. **If you are separated unto God, then you can't bow to peer pressure.** Let's think about the children of Israel for a moment. Remember them? The book of Exodus in the Old Testament tells their story. Remember how Joseph was sold by his brothers and ended up in the land of Egypt? Then, his whole family came to Egypt to live. That family grew in size until they became over 1 million people living in the land of Egypt. They became slaves over a period of 400 years. They were DAILY pressured to make a certain amount of bricks and if they didn't, they were beaten. They were so pressured that they started crying out for deliverance. God heard them and sent them Moses.

Moses brought them God's Word. Through God's mighty acts on their behalf, the Israelites walked out of Egypt. As long as they were in Egypt, they couldn't be separated unto God because Egypt wouldn't allow them. God had to get them OUT of Egypt, out from under that pressure so that He could teach them about Him. All those years of living under that pressure had robbed them of much of the knowledge of God and what He wanted for them.

The same goes for you. God wants you separated unto Him so that He can teach you about His ways and about what He has for you. **If you're constantly being swayed by peer pressure, you can't hear God. If you can't hear God, then you'll miss the mark.** You'll miss walking in those steps that God already has laid out for you.

Let's look at some more of God's Word about hitting the mark of God.

Philippians 3:13, 14 (This is Paul talking here.)
". . .I am still not all I should be but I am bringing all my energies to bear on this one thing: Forgetting the past and looking forward to what lies ahead, I strain to reach the end of the race and receive the prize for which God is calling us up to heaven because of what Christ Jesus did for us."

Here come the questions again.

- **What was the ONE thing upon which Paul said he was focusing?**
- **What was he STRAINING to reach?**
- **Why was he STRAINING to reach it?**
- **Who made it possible for him or us to reach it?**

The answers are all there. Let's look at another verse.

Hebrews 12:1
". . .let us strip off anything that slows us down or holds us back, and especially those sins that wrap themselves so tightly around our feet and trip us up; and let us run with patience the particular race that God has set before us."

Here are some more questions.

- **What is it we're supposed to strip off?**
- **What kind of race is it we're supposed to run?**

Does that give you the picture of a passive Christian? Does that give you the picture of a Christian who just sits down and says to himself, "I'll just sit here and take whatever comes my way"? Do you know what a passive Christian is? LAZY. Yes, I said lazy. **Lazy Christians don't run their PARTICULAR race.** Lazy Christians don't find out God's will for their lives and then follow it. Lazy Christians just sit and yield to peer pressure and anything else that comes along that grabs their attention.

Does God love lazy Christians? Yes, He loves them but He doesn't love what they're doing. They're cheating God. You heard me. They're cheating God! They're like a person who goes to work for another person and then instead of cleaning the shelves or sweeping the floor or whatever they were hired to do, they just go into a corner to sit and read a book or sleep. They weren't hired to do that. They were hired to do the job the employer said they were to do and when they don't do that, they are CHEATING the employer out of a day's work.

Whenever you or I do not pursue God to find out what we're supposed to be doing, we are CHEATING HIM out of a day's work. When you or I do not pursue doing what He has shown us to do, we are CHEATING HIM out of a day's work. When you or I continually yield to peer pressure to dress like that, talk like that, or act like that, we are CHEATING GOD of what is due Him.

Jesus paid a heavy price for you to run a PARTICULAR race, and He didn't shed His blood, die on the cross, and rise from the dead for you to continually yield to peer pressure. **The peer pressure race is not the particular race you're supposed to run.** It's not in the book where God has recorded all the days of your life. You will not find where God has written down that you will yield to peer pressure during a certain period of time. NEVER!!!

The Tortoise and the Hare

Have you ever heard the story of the tortoise and the hare? It's an old story but has an important meaning. I'm changing it a little and adding some elements of peer pressure to it.

Our first contender for this race is the hare or another name would be a rabbit. Think about the natural qualities of rabbits for a moment. They have the ability to run or hop fast. In fact, that is their natural way of getting from one place to another.

Our second contender for this race is the tortoise or turtle. When you see a turtle, what is your first thought? Slow. He moves slow. Everything about him is slow moving.

Now, the thought of these two running a race is almost ludicrous. Of course, you would think that the rabbit would win because of his natural ability to hop fast and the turtle's natural ability to move slowly. Why that rabbit would have finished the race and finished his dinner by the time the turtle ever got close to the finish line. This is what you would think.

Here is where I am going to add some different elements to the story and give these two the personalities of humans.

Coming up to the starting line of the race is Harrison Hare. All of his "friends," which are many, are on the sidelines cheering him on to victory. Harrison is a party rabbit. He attends every party anyone has. He receives invitations to every one because he is the life of the party. Everyone likes him because he doesn't stand for anything and will become whatever they want him to become so they will like him. No one ever feels threatened by Harrison's presence at a party. They never feel ashamed that what they might be doing just might be wrong because whatever it is, Harrison just joins in and participates right along with them. Harrison is a fashion dresser, too. Are the styles decent? Do they cover parts of the body that need to be covered? Doesn't matter. Harrison wears them anyway. After all, he wants to fit in and will compromise decency to do it. He talks like all his "friends." He curses just like them. If he walks up to a group of boys or girls and they are using God's name in vain or using foul language of any kind, he just adapts his speech to fit right in with them. What if tattoos are the "in" thing? Harrison goes down to the tattoo parlor and has one or more inked in on his body. What about the earring in the ear for boys? Now, do you think Harrison would be left out of that? Of course not. He goes to a jewelry store or somewhere that pierces ears and gets his ear pierced and slips an earring right through there. He has to fit in. **He just can't exist without fitting in.** His goal in life is to "fit in" with the rest of the crowd. Does he ever consider that God might have a plan for his

33

life? NEVER. He's too busy trying to please all his "friends."

Here is our second contender, Terrance Tortoise. Terrance doesn't have a long list of friends, but the friends he does have are really good friends and trustworthy. Terrance knows that if he has a problem, one of his friends or all of them will be there for him and he will do the same for them. They aren't focused on trying to "fit in" with anyone. They are focused on pleasing God and helping each other stay on God's pathway. All of them attend church and read their Bible daily. They spend time talking about God and have a heart desirous of God. They have parties but they don't compromise their Christian values in any way. Terrance is a smart dresser but a conservative dresser. He doesn't wear clothes just because they are the fashion of the day. He critically examines them and determines if what he is wearing is pleasing to God and if it covers his body the way it should. This requires some effort on his part because the stores like to stock what the world says is the fashion of the day, and sometimes, he has to hunt to find those quality pieces of clothing. Terrance has dedicated his body to the Lord and doesn't cover it with tattoos nor wear an earring in his ear just because someone started that fashion statement. He isn't a member of a lot of clubs because he needs time for church activities and time to spend with God. He knows how to appropriate his time so that God is always first. Terrance doesn't care a thing about what others think of him or if they talk about him. His relationship with God is secure. He doesn't need to "fit in" with any group in order to be happy. He doesn't need THEIR approval. They can try to use peer pressure on him all they want but they are just wasting their time. Terrance knows that God has a plan for his life because he has found in God's Word where it is so. That's his goal in life, to find out God's plan for him and walk in it.

The two individuals stand at the starting line in racing position. Harrison is cocky and showing off to all his friends on the sidelines. Really, Harrison is just being Harrison, not serious about anything. He goes into this race NEVER considering that he just might lose. Terrance stands there with determination and quietness that he is going to run this race to please God, not man. His friends are on the sidelines, too, and they are yelling, "Go for it, Terrance! We're with you and God's on your side!"

The starting pistol cracks its sound through the air and the two are off. Harrison zips up the track and thinks, "Take that, Terrance! Eat my dust!" His friends run alongside screaming, "Go—go---go!!! You've got old 'Tortoise Shell' beat!"

Harrison relishes every word. It feeds his ego. He puffs up more with pride if that's possible. As his chest expands, he thinks, "I am truly un-beatable." Looking back, he doesn't see any sign of Terrance. Then, his friends start yelling, "Hey,

Harrison, come on over here and take a break. You've got plenty of time."

Harrison looks around and thinks about it for a moment. Since he didn't spot Terrance anywhere, he steps off the race track and goes to join his friends. They party; they eat; they drink; and they play games. Every time Harrison starts back to the racetrack, his friends talk him out of it. "You've got P-L-E-N-T-Y of time," they assure him with drunken slurs. "Have another drink."

Before Harrison realizes it, time has slipped away. The sun has gone down to the treetops. He looks at his watch and hours have passed. Throwing his drink aside, he staggers back to the racetrack, trying to catch up with Terrance. Way in the distance he can see the finish line. There are people cheering and waving banners. A big yellow ribbon is stretched across the finish line. Harrison just knows he can make it and all those people are hollering for him. He decides to turn up his speed a notch, but he is buzzed by the alcoholic drinks he has been consuming. His mind says, "Speed up," but he just can't get his body to comply. He doesn't feel good, either. His stomach is upset and his head is fuzzy because he has eaten and drunk too much when he should have been finishing the race. His body is slowing him down.

To his dismay, he watches as the slow, plodding figure of Terrance Tortoise approaches the finish line. He blinks several times trying to clear his blurred eyes. No, what he is seeing is true. Terrance Tortoise is crossing the finish line and receiving his award. The crowd cheers and runs to hug Terrance.

What happened to Harrison? What kind of choices did Harrison make that prevented him from finishing the race? Was it the fault of the person who designed the race that Harrison didn't finish? You can answer all these questions. Look at your own life. **What is keeping YOU from finishing the race God has called you to run?** Don't use the excuse that you don't know what that race is. You start by asking God and turning yourself over to Him. You put Him first by reading His Word, spending time in prayer, spending time with other Christians, and desiring most of all to please God in every part of your life. What is keeping you from doing those things?

The Foolish vs. the Wise

Here's another story of peer pressure from the Bible. I'm going to quote the whole passage so you will see it right in front of your eyes. Usually, we read this passage in the context of Jesus returning to earth, but in this case, I want you to see it through the eyes of peer pressure. I am quoting this from the Amplified translation of the Bible.

Matthew 25:1-13
"Then the kingdom of heaven shall be likened to ten virgins who took their lamps and went to meet the bridegroom.

Five of them were foolish—thoughtless, without forethought; and five were wise—sensible, intelligent and prudent.

For when the foolish took their lamps, they did not take any [extra] oil with them;

But the wise took flasks of oil along with them [also] with their lamps.

While the bridegroom lingered and was slow in coming, they all began nodding their heads and fell asleep.

But at midnight there was a shout, Behold, the bridegroom! Go out to meet him!

Then all those virgins got up and put their own lamps in order.

And the foolish said to the wise, Give us some of your oil, for our lamps are going out.

But the wise replied, There will not be enough for us and for you; go instead to the dealers and buy for yourselves.

But while they were gone away to buy, the bridegroom came, and those who were prepared went in with him to the marriage feast; and the door was shut.

Later the other virgins also came, and said, Lord, Lord, open [the door] to us!

But He replied, I solemnly declare to you, I do not know you—I am not acquainted with you.

Watch therefore—give strict attention and be cautious and active—for you know neither the day nor the hour when the Son of man will come."

Read back over this passage again and see if you can spot the peer pressure. I love the way the Amplified translation describes the foolish virgins. Think of them as foolish people—male or female. They were called foolish because they were

- **THOUGHTLESS**
- **WITHOUT FORETHOUGHT**

Think about those the two words "thoughtless" and "forethought" for a moment. What do you think they mean? Obviously, "thoughtless" means without any thought because the ending of "less" takes away from the word "thought." Right? The word "forethought" means giving some thinking and consideration about something beforehand

39

because the prefix "fore" adds to the word "thought" here. Right? With just those definitions, could you describe what these five foolish people were like, character wise? Can you think of any people like that? Don't name them. Just think about them for a moment. What makes them like that? What characteristics do they exhibit which cause you to immediately think of them in comparison to the five foolish people here?

These five people mentioned in Matthew 13:2 did not plan, did not think about what they were doing, and were only living for the moment. They didn't plan to run a race. They took each day as it came and just lived that day however they wanted to or however the day dictated to them that they should live. They never sought God about what they were supposed to do. They never considered serving Him daily so that they would be prepared for anything that He needed them to do.

Now, look at the five wise virgins or the five wise people. These five were called wise because they were

- **SENSIBLE**
- **INTELLIGENT**
- **PRUDENT**

Their senses were not dulled by partying, alcohol drinking or drug use. They had chosen to pursue God and His ways which sharpened the intelligence that God had already given them. Through their serving God, they had become wise because God directed their steps through His Word and through the Holy Spirit Who dwelled inside them. They knew to prepare for the future and that knowledge came from knowing God.

Notice, also in this passage of Scripture that the ten were ALL virgins but five of them were foolish and five were wise. Did you know that you can be a Christian and never pursue God for His perfect will in your life? Did you know that you can be a Christian and yield to peer pressure?

I'm not talking about sinning here. Sinning is another thing and sin cuts you off from God's life. If you do sin, **RUN TO GOD, NOT FROM HIM.** Ask forgiveness and get back on track with Him. I'm talking about whether or not as a Christian you seek God's PERFECT will for your life**. Peer pressure doesn't want you or anyone to seek God's perfect will because God's will takes you out from under the thumb of peer pressure's will.**

Look at the staunchness of the five wise people when approached by peer pressure. The five foolish people didn't prepare for the bridegroom's appearance. We could say that they didn't prepare to finish the race on time. They did all THEY WANTED and what they perceived THEY HAD to do for the moment. It wasn't enough. They didn't take extra oil with them just in case they had to

41

wait a little longer than necessary. They started out looking like good strong Christians, but couldn't keep looking that way because they didn't prepare for it.

Once the cry went out that it was time for them to finish the race, guess what? Their oil had run out and they didn't have any to complete the race. What were they going to do? They tried to get the wise people to give some of their oil to them. They pressured them, "Give us some of your oil. Can't you see our lamps are going out?" Now, the wise people could have said, "Oh, here take some of ours," but if they had, none of them would have finished the race. Besides, this race was for each one individually. Each one was required to prepare for the race and run it.

When the five foolish people saw that the wise weren't going to yield to their peer pressure, they had to do something about finding some more oil. They left to go buy some and while they were gone, the bridegroom came and the five wise people went in with Him.

After the door was shut, the five foolish people came back and knocked on the door wanting to come in. The bridegroom wouldn't open the door to them because the time limit was up. **See, there is a time for you to run the particular race that God has set before you and throw aside the peer pressure that would try to trip you.** Your time is now and your time to finish is when God says and not before that time. God never tells you to run a while, take a rest, and then run some more. You are on this racetrack until the finish. It is a DAILY running and a DAILY seeking God. You have to be like the five wise people and not give in to peer pressure that would try to pull you aside. You don't want to miss anything God has for you. **Everything He has is for your good and it is always good, never harmful.**

ಙ ~ ೞ

Review Questions for Chapter 2

1. What is peer pressure always trying to take away from you? Explain.

2. Give the Scripture reference in which God says that He has a plan for your life.

3. If you want to follow God's plan for your life, what do you have to use?

4. Explain what you believe is the difference between being "God-conscious" and "peer-conscious."

5. What keeps you from bowing to peer pressure?

6. Describe a lazy Christian.

7. Using one sentence or one phrase, describe Harrison Hare. Do the same for Terrance Tortoise.

8. Why doesn't peer pressure want you to seek God's will for your life?

Chapter 3
Make the Decision –
Refuse to Bow

As Meshach and Abednego stood talking with one another, discussing their day's activities, Abednego glanced up to see a figure running toward them. He could tell the person was definitely in a hurry and looked as if he had an important message to deliver.

As the figure drew closer, Meshach recognized him. "That's Shadrach!" he exclaimed.

"You're right," Abednego answered. "Wonder why he's in such a rush?"

"Hey Shadrach!" Abednego shouted and waved his hand in greeting.

"Let-me-catch-my-breath," Shadrach said in a halting voice.

"Sit down. You look beat," Meshach said as he patted him on the back.

"Whew! That was a run," Shadrach finally said in a more normal voice. "I have important news. Have you two heard what King Nebuchadnezzar has done?"

Meshach and Abednego looked at one another as if to say, "Do you know?" and then looked back at Shadrach with expectant faces.

"No," Abednego answered for the two of them, "we don't."

"Well, wait until you hear this. King Nebuchadnezzar has built a golden statue 90 feet tall and nine feet wide in the plain of Dura," Shadrach explained. "Not only that, but he has sent for all the chief officials to come to the dedication of it. If you haven't received your invitation yet, you will. He hasn't left anyone out."

Shadrach, Meshach and Abednego were part of the chief officials. When Daniel was promoted (see Daniel 2:48, 49) he asked the king to set these three men over the affairs of the province of Babylon. That made them three of the chief officials.

"What do you think he plans to do with that statue?" Meshach asked. Really, he was thinking out loud. "Surely he doesn't expect people to bow to that thing."

"Sounds like an idol to me," Abednego answered. He had been thinking also. It was clear that all three of them were thinking along the same line of thought. They served God and God had plainly stated in the Ten Commandments (Exodus 20:3, 4)

"You may worship no other god than me. You shall not make yourselves any idols: any images resembling animals, birds, or fish. You must never bow to an image or worship it in any way; for I, the Lord your God, am very possessive. I will not share your affection with any other god!"

"Let's decide here and now what we're going to do if we get there and he expects us to bow to that thing," Meshach said with a voice of authority.

The other two nodded in agreement. "We're not bowing," Shadrach firmly stated. "There isn't any question to be considered here. We're not bowing to any man-made idol, even if we have to die for it. I'd rather die obeying God than disobey Him just to save my earthly life."

The three men decided to travel together to the dedication. By this time, all three men had received their official "invitation" to the dedication. As they approached the area, they saw the enormous statue looming in the distance. Many people were traveling toward it, while others who had been there for a while, were standing and gazing in awe at the tall giant of gold. There was a buzz of voices as people talked with one another about the statue and possibly why the king had it built.

Shadrach, Meshach, and Abednego stood there silently and listened to the different conversations.

"I can see why the king had it built here. Where else could he have put it?"

"I've never seen anything so big."

"Why did he build it?"

"I wonder how long it took to make it."

The conversations went on and on until a herald stood up to read the proclamation from the king. All of them, Shadrach, Meshach and Abednego included, were about to find out why they were there.

Here is what the herald said:

"O people of all nations and languages, this is the king's command: When the band strikes up, you are to fall flat on the ground to worship

King Nebuchadnezzar's golden statue; anyone who refuses to obey will immediately be thrown into a flaming furnace."

Shadrach, Meshach and Abednego looked at one another and smiled. It was not a sarcastic smile. It was a KNOWING smile of joy. The decision had been made. **They weren't bowing**.

At that moment, the music started playing. With one fell swoop, all the standing figures collapsed to the floor on their faces in a worshipful bow to that golden statue. That is, **all except three.** In the midst of all those face-to-the-floor figures, three remained erect.

Shadrach heard this noise to the right of him coming from a position around his feet, "P-s-s-s-t!" He followed the sound with his eyes and ears and saw someone he didn't know on his face in a bowed position. This person loudly whispered, "Aren't you bowing?" Shadrach shook his head to indicate that he wasn't. The man quickly turned his head as if making sure no one saw him talking to the rebels.

However, there were spies who were watching. Apparently, they had been bowing and watching from under their arms for anyone they could tattle on and possibly receive a reward for doing so. These spies were some of the officials. They rushed to the king as soon as they could and reported the following,

"Your Majesty! You made a law that everyone must fall down and worship the golden statue when the band begins to play, and that anyone who refuses will be thrown into a flaming furnace. But there are some Jews out there— Shadrach, Meshach, and Abednego, whom you have put in charge of Babylonian affairs—who have defied you, refusing to serve your gods or to worship the golden statue you set up."

This fire to which they were referring was not a little campfire. This was a huge furnace in which people could stand. The men assigned to that part of the dedication had been working for days gathering up enough wood to heat that thing in case it was needed. Once this fire was heated up enough, it could handle huge logs being thrown into it.

Once King Nebuchadnezzar heard that report, he flew into a rage. Without thinking about what he was doing, he ordered that Shadrach, Meshach and Abednego be brought before him. How dare they disobey him!

The three men were brought before the king. "Is it true what I hear, Shadrach, Meshach and Abednego? Are you refusing to serve my gods or to worship my golden statue? I'm going to give you one more chance. When the music plays, if you fall down and worship the statue as I commanded, everything will be okay. But hear this, if you don't, all three of you will be thrown into the fiery furnace within the same hour. And who is going to deliver you then? What god can deliver you out of my hands?"

Here is what they replied. They didn't have to go huddle about this. Remember they had already made the decision before they went.

"O Nebuchadnezzar, we are not worried about what will happen to us. If we are thrown into the flaming furnace, our God is able to deliver us; and he will deliver us out of your hand, Your Majesty. But if he doesn't, please understand, sir, that even then we will never under any circumstance serve your gods or worship the golden statue you have erected."

King Nebuchadnezzar's face turned beet red with anger. His countenance changed from one of a pleading look for them to obey him to one of furious wrath. He issued a command that the furnace be heated SEVEN TIMES hotter than usual. Then he called for some of the strongest men in his army to bind the three men so that they couldn't possibly escape. These men were also commanded to throw them into the fire.

The soldiers bound the men as commanded and carried them to the fire, but as they were throwing them in, the flames leaped out and killed the soldiers. Shadrach, Meshach, and Abednego were thrown in bound with ropes. They should have been burnt to a crisp right where they were.

51

Everyone around was shocked at the death of the soldiers. While they were still talking about that, the king suddenly leaped from his chair. He stared at the fire as if he were looking at something unusual. With a quizzical look upon his face, he turned to some of the men around him and asked, "Didn't we throw three men into the fiery furnace?"

The men looked at one another as if to say, "What's wrong with the king?" but they knew better than to say anything like that. Instead, they agreed with him. "Yes, King, we did."

Then with a sweeping flourish of his hand, King Nebuchadnezzar pointed his finger toward the fire and shouted, "WELL---LOOK!!! I see FOUR men, unbound, walking around in there and they aren't even hurt by the flames. The fourth one looks like a god."

King Nebuchadnezzar walked as close as he could get to the furnace without being consumed by the heat and the leaping flames. He shouted across the fiery tongues of fire, "Shadrach, Meshach and Abednego, servants of the Most High God, come out of the fire! Come here to me!"

Everyone there watched in amazement as the three men stepped through the flames and continued walking until they were a safe distance from the furnace. The people crowded around them looking for evidence that they had been in a fire. Surely, there must be a burn somewhere on their clothing. Some of them asked to see their hands. There wasn't a burn mark anywhere. Others were coming up and sniffing around their clothing and hair trying to smell smoke. There wasn't any. Not one hair was singed or burnt. Not one piece of their clothing was burnt AND they didn't stink of smoke. They weren't even warm.

God had sent an angel to rescue them. Then Nebuchadnezzar said these words to them and all those standing around,

"Blessed be the God of Shadrach, Meshach, and Abednego, for he sent his angel to deliver his trusting servants when they defied the king's commandment, and were willing to die rather than serve or worship any god except their own. Therefore, I make this decree, that any person of any nation, language, or religion who speaks a word against the God of Shadrach, Meshach, and Abednego shall be torn limb from limb and his house knocked into a heap of rubble. For no other God can do what this one does."

After this, the king promoted all three men and they prospered there.

This true story comes from the book of Daniel chapter 3. I have written it in my own words to enliven it and I have quoted at times directly from The Living Bible.

Did you understand the message this story is telling? These three men made the decision BEFORE they ever stepped into that situation that they weren't bowing. No, they didn't know exactly what was going to happen, but they knew whatever it was, they weren't going to disappoint God and turn their backs on HIM.

Jesus is all about making decisions. When we accept Him as Lord of our lives, we make the decision to do that. By the way, if you haven't done that, pray this prayer right now. It's simple and it's easy.

Heavenly Father, I believe that You sent Jesus to this earth to die for my sin. I also believe that You raised Him from the dead for me. Jesus, I ask You into my heart this moment. I turn my life over to You. Come be Lord of my life.

Now, you're a Christian. You're a follower of Christ and you have prepared yourself to receive wisdom from God's Word.

Jesus made a statement to a group of people in Luke chapter 9 and verse 62 about making a decision.

". . . Anyone who lets himself be distracted from the work I plan for him is not fit for the Kingdom of God."

Those are strong words for anyone to hear. Here is what the Amplified translation of the Bible says.

". . .No one who puts his hand to the plow and looks back [to the things behind] is fit for the kingdom of God."

That word "fit" is used in an interesting way. Have you ever tried to "fit" something into something else? Think back to your pre-school days. I never went to pre-school. My first experience with school of any kind was first grade. In those days, children were not expected to go to pre-school. When I taught 4 and 5 year old children, though, sometimes we put puzzles together. These were simple puzzles for older children, but for smaller children they took some effort and some thought. The pieces were big but they were cut to fit EXACTLY into a certain place on that puzzle board. I watched as some quickly put them in place while others had difficulty. They might try and try to fit a piece in but it just wasn't cut to fit that place. Surely you know that you can't fit a round piece of puzzle in a square hole nor can you fit a square piece of puzzle in a round hole. They weren't made for each other and THEY WON'T FIT.

When you become a Christian, you place yourself in a position to receive revelation knowledge from God about His Word. Just by asking God, you can receive all the wisdom you need about a situation. Your spirit man has been reborn and he can take in spiritual information that as a non-Christian, you just can't handle. HOWEVER, that does not make you "fit" for the kingdom of God. **What makes you fit is your CONTINUAL pressing into God.** What do I mean by that? That means that you are continually seeking God. You are devoted to Him. You don't allow ANYTHING to come between you and Him. You read your Bible. You do everything you know to do to please God. Your every thought is how you can please God today. You shudder at the thought of displeasing Him one little bit. If it means that you lose friends over it, then so be it. You have made the decision that you're not allowing anything to come between you and your relationship with God.

When you have the attitude of, "I'm going to serve God no matter what anyone thinks about me," then you are making yourself "fit" for the kingdom of God. You have made the decision that you will not be distracted by anything. Being fit means that you allow God to fit you into **HIS** plan for you. You don't force it and you don't allow anyone else to force you into a plan other than God's plan for you. **Peer pressure will try to force you off God's plan.** Your peers will try to use you to satisfy THEIR wants and needs and that is not God's way. You weren't designed to fit into anything but God's plan for you. When you're in God's perfect plan, you won't find yourself fighting against anything God has for you. You'll fit into place just like a puzzle piece fits into the place that has been cut for it. You have been "cut and shaped" just to fit the place God has designed for you.

Let's go back to the word "distracted" for a moment. **Peer pressure is a distracter.** While you're trying to follow God, peer pressure is screaming at you to come this way or go that way. Think of it in this manner. I'm going to use the example of a dog. I had a dog named Rex when I was a child, so I'm going to name this dog, Rex. Let's say that Rex has a bag of money in his mouth. That bag of money belongs to one of the people in a group who is Rex's owner. Ten people are standing around wanting that money. They know that if they try to take it from him, he'll turn and run and they may never catch him. So, they start yelling his name and trying to get him to come to them. Rex knows his owner. He has spotted him, but every time he starts toward this person, the others start screaming his name. "Rex, here boy, come over here!" They're kneeling on the ground, trying to look inviting to him and whistling at him. As they call his name, they are moving their hands in a calling motion to him. "Here Rex. Come here, boy. I've got a treat for you." Some of them are holding up bones trying to entice him to come to them. Rex just doesn't know what to do. To whom does he go? His head jerks back and forth between the people. He is being distracted from his purpose.

That's what peer pressure will do to you. As you start toward God, peer pressure will attempt to DISTRACT you from what God has called you to do. You have to refuse to look at the ones causing the peer pressure. Jesus said you don't look back to the things behind. We could say it this way. We don't look back to those things that might look inviting to us for a season. We don't look back to those things that might make us think we fit in better. We don't look back to those things that we think or anyone else thinks might make us have more fun. Whose description of fun are you believing? **God is fun.** YES, I said GOD IS FUN. Peer pressure tells you that He isn't, but remember what I said earlier—PEER PRESSURE LIES. Peer pressure doesn't know a thing about God and doesn't want to know. **Peer pressure is intent on making peer pressure feel good.** Do you know that peer pressure can't feel good unless it has someone over whom to lord itself? Peer pressure ALWAYS requires that another person be involved or it isn't peer pressure. Take away the people and peer pressure doesn't have any effect.

God has a perfect plan for you. Your steps are already laid out, but what happens when you yield to peer pressure? Whose pathway do you step over on when you yield to peer pressure? Are you on God's pathway any longer? You know the answer to that.

Don't you know God is smart and He's way smarter than you? He designed this earth. Look at Isaiah chapter 40 and verses 12 through 15.

"Who else has held the oceans in his hands and measured off the heavens with his ruler? Who else knows the weight of all the earth and weighs the mountains and the hills? Who can advise the Spirit of the Lord or be his teacher or give him counsel? Has he ever needed anyone's advice? Did he need instruction as to what is right and best? No, for all the peoples of the world are nothing in comparison with him—they are but a drop in the bucket, dust on the scales. He picks up the islands as though they had no weight at all."

Peer pressure thinks it is always right. Why would it be pressuring you if it didn't think it was right? You have to look at where peer pressure is getting its wisdom. It isn't coming from God because God never pressures anyone. God never intended for man to have dominion over other men. I'm talking here about the species of man which includes women. I'm not talking about people who have authority over others in positions that require that such as jobs, schools, churches, etc. I'm talking about when men want to enslave another person to get them to do what THEY want. They bully them or taunt them to get them to do what they want. That isn't God's way.

ॐ ~ ॐ

Review Questions for Chapter 3

1. From Shadrach, Meshach and Abednego's actions, how would you describe their character? How do you think they would respond to peer pressure of any kind? What decision did they make as a group?

2. Give the Scripture reference in which Jesus warned about distraction.

3. What makes you fit for the kingdom of God? Explain your answer.

4. Consider this scenario. You are walking down a road. God has told you that this road is THE road upon which you are to walk. As you walk down this road, you encounter peer pressure. What will peer pressure's reaction be upon seeing you?

5. What does peer pressure require to be peer pressure?

6. What does peer pressure think?

Chapter 4
Just Turn and Walk Away

"Angie, are you coming Saturday night?" Angie finished stuffing a book into her school locker and turned toward the direction of the voice of her friend, Julia. Julia and she weren't close friends, but they did occasionally spend time together.

"Yes," Angie replied. "What time do you want me there?"

"Oh, just come around 6," Julia said. "My parents are going out at 7 and should be back around 10. It will be just us girls. We will have a really good time."

"Us girls" referred to the other girls Julia had invited to the party—Emily, Natasha, Rosita and Jackie.

"I'll be there," Angie said as she shut her locker door. "I'm really looking forward to it. See you then."

Fifteen-year-old Angie was a Christian and had been for about 6 years. She accepted Jesus as her Lord and Savior when she was nine years old. Since that time, she had grown much in the Lord. She loved God with all her heart and she did not want to ever displease Him in any way. She also loved her parents. She was blessed that both her parents were Christians and had taken her to church since she was big enough to be carried to church. Christianity to Angie was not "lip service." She didn't just talk Christianity; she lived it.

Saturday night arrived and after Angie dressed for the party which was to start in about 30 minutes, she went downstairs to wait for her mother. Her mother was driving her to Julia's house.

Angie's mother wasn't worried because she knew all the girls who would be attending and she knew Julia and her parents. All of them attended the same church, and the girls all shared the same church school classroom.

Angie and her mother climbed into the car and within minutes were at Julia's house. As Angie was leaving the car, she turned to her mother and said, "Thanks, Mom!"

"I'll be here at 10 to pick you up," her mother reminded her.

"Okay," Angie answered.

With a final word, her mother said, "Have a good time," and drove off.

Julia was standing at the door waiting for her. She had seen them drive up. "Come on in! The others haven't arrived yet."

Angie stepped inside and spoke to Julia's parents and then the two girls went into the Family Room to await the arrival of the other girls. All of them arrived within just a few minutes of Angie's arrival.

Julia and her mother had prepared homemade pizzas for everyone. They had made it more interesting by preparing the toppings and leaving them in separate bowls so everyone could "make" their own pizza. Each person could pick out the toppings they wanted and pile them on the pizza dough prepared just for them which already had the pizza sauce on it. They decided to eat around 7 PM and had great fun preparing their own pizzas. As they were popping their pizzas into the oven, Julia's parents left instructions for Julia about where to reach them and then they left. They had assured her that they would be back by 10 PM.

Around 8 PM, Julia hollered from the kitchen, "I've got a surprise for all of you."

The girls looked at one another not having any idea what kind of surprise she had in mind. They thought Julia or her mother might have made some delicious dessert since all of them were partial to sweets.

Julia walked into the room with one hand behind her back and the other hand holding six paper cups. She handed the cups to Angie and instructed her to pass them out to everyone.

Angie did as she was told, but at the same time, she wondered if this were some kind of game they were going to play. Maybe they were going to throw something and everyone try to catch it with their cups. She just couldn't imagine.

When each person had her cup, they all looked at Julia with expectant faces. Julia brought her other hand from behind her back and in it was a bottle of liquor, an alcoholic beverage. Angie didn't know anything about liquor except for empty bottles she had occasionally seen on the street. Plus, she had an aunt and uncle who like to indulge in it, and she had seen bottles similar to what Julia was holding in their home bar which they always kept locked. She couldn't imagine where Julia had obtained a bottle like that and she certainly wasn't going to ask.

"We're going to experiment," Julia excitedly said as if she were teaching a class of willing students. "We're going to drink and see how long it takes to get a 'buzz.' We'll stop before we actually get drunk because I don't want my parents or your parents finding out about it. This is going to be our secret."

Angie sat there stunned. She really didn't want to believe what she was seeing. The other girls were saying almost in unison, "A-l-l-right!!! Let's get started!"

Angie watched as they eagerly held out their cups for a trip down "Buzz Lane." Instead of Angie holding out her cup with them, she crumpled her cup in her hand and walked over to the trashcan, lifted the lid, threw in the crumpled cup, and closed the lid.

"What are you doing?" Emily asked.

"Yeah, Angie, don't have the stomach for it?" Natasha added sarcastically.

With those initial remarks, the others chimed in with equally harsh statements. They even threatened to make up stories on her and spread them over school if she didn't participate or if she told on them.

Angie looked at them in disbelief. She wanted to go outside and look at the house number because surely this wasn't the house of her friend. Surely she had wandered into a stranger's house. No, she was in the house of her friend. She knew all these girls or at least she THOUGHT she knew them. When presented with one temptation, all of them melted and became as one with it. Not only that, but they all, as a group, TURNED ON HER.

Angie grabbed her purse and pulled out her cell phone. After turning it on, she started dialing her parents' number. At this action, Julia's eyes flashed fire. She ran over to Angie and tried to jerk the cell phone from Angie's hands. "Give me that!" she spat out with fury.

"No," Angie calmly but authoritatively said. "It's not yours." Then she laid the phone down for a moment and looked at each one of them. "Let me tell you something. I'm a Christian and I don't do anything that I know will displease my Heavenly Father. Not only does this displease Him, but it works against the health of my body. My body is the temple of the Holy Spirit. I was bought with the price of Jesus' blood and so were each one of you. I'm calling my mother to come pick me up. I am walking out that door and you will not try to stop me."

"Are you going to tell?" Rosita asked.

"I'm going to tell my mother and then it will be up to her and my father whether or not they tell your parents."

With that final word, Angie dialed the number, told her mother she needed to be picked up, and then went outside to wait for her.

This is just a story that I made up but it could easily happen to anyone, even you. It might be a different circumstance but the pressure is the same.

- **How are you going to deal with it?**
- **What are you going to do?**
- **What are you going to say?**
- **Will you stay and participate or will you get up and walk away?**

Jesus walked away. The book of Luke records an incident where Jesus was speaking the truth, and the religious leaders just didn't want to hear it. In fact, they became so mad that they wanted to kill Him. You can read the whole story starting with Luke chapter 4 and verse 16. I'm going to start with verse 28 and go through verse 30.

"These remarks stung them to fury; and jumping up, they mobbed him and took him to the edge of the hill on which the city was built, to push him over the cliff. But he walked away through the crowd and left them."

Now, I'm going to quote this from the Amplified translation so you can see just how serious this really was. This translation goes into a little more detail.

"When they heard these things, all the people in the synagogue were filled with rage.

And rising up they pushed and drove Him out of the town, and (laying hold of Him) they led Him to the (projecting) upper part of the hill on which their town was built, that they might hurl Him headlong down [over the cliff].

But passing through their midst, He went on His way."

Did you notice that verse 28 said that ALL the people were filled with rage. All of them. Not just one but ALL of them. Not one person to whom He was speaking did not get mad. As a group, they got up and started pushing and shoving Him in a particular direction. They knew exactly where they were taking Him. They had a plan. Apparently, they had shoved people off that cliff before or had seen people fall off or be pushed. There was a spit of land that stuck out over the hill, and it must have been a high hill. They pressured Jesus to get to that point so they could pick Him up and throw Him over the cliff and be done with Him.

I know that this is an extreme situation and you may not relate this to the topic of peer pressure but I do. Let's look at through the eyes of peer pressure. These people, who were His peers, were upset that He had gone against their way of thinking and doing. They pressured Him to go where they wanted Him to go. But, Jesus didn't follow the plan THEY had laid out for Him. When it came to the crucial part of their plan, **Jesus just turned and walked away from them.** Actually, He walked right through them and they couldn't lift a finger to stop Him.

In situations involving peer pressure, you have a choice. **You can yield to the pressure or you can walk away from it.** Proverbs is full of instruction about staying out of trouble and not yielding to pressure from others to involve yourself in it. The first thing God expects you to do is reverence Him. The second thing is to obey your parents. If you determine that you are going to reverence God, then you will obey your parents. If you obey your parents and listen to their instruction, you will stay out of trouble. Look at these verses.

Proverbs 1:7-9
"How does a man become wise? The first step is to trust and reverence the Lord! Only fools refuse to be taught. Listen to your father and mother. What you learn from them will stand you in good stead; it will gain you many honors."

This chapter goes on from here to set up a scenario of possible peer pressure and how you're supposed to respond to it.

Proverbs 1:10-19
**"If young toughs tell you, 'Come and join us'—
turn your back on them! 'We'll hide and rob
and kill,' they say. 'Good or bad, we'll treat
them all alike. And the loot we'll get! All kinds
of stuff! Come on, throw in your lot with us;
we'll split with you in equal shares.'**

**Don't do it, son! Stay far from men like that,
for crime is their way of life, and murder is
their specialty.**

**When a bird sees a trap being set, it stays away,
but not these men; they trap themselves! They
lay a booby trap for their own lives. Such is the
fate of all who live by violence and murder.
They will die a violent death."**

I want to quote a section of that passage from
the Amplified translation. Watch for "peer
pressure" words.

Verse 14
**"Throw in your lot among us [they insist], and
be a sworn brother and comrade; let us all have
one purse in common."**

This translation shows how insistent they were.
What is insistence? It is pressure. From where was
it coming in this verse? From his peers. They want
him to be a sworn brother and comrade. In other
words, they want him to join their gang, become a
blood brother with them so that he will never want

to tell on them for anything they do. They want to involve him so deeply in their activities that he will feel pressure to stay with them, and that pressure will be so strong that he will never leave them.

What does verse 15 say about that? Again, from the Amplified translation, here it is.

"My son, do not walk in the way with them, restrain your foot from their path;"

If the instruction is "do not walk," that means that you have a choice of walking and you have the power to NOT walk. God's Word never tells you to NOT do something when you don't have a choice about not doing it. Do you understand that? If God says, "Don't steal!" then you have a choice of whether or not you steal. Again, if you are instructed to "restrain your foot," that means you have the choice and the power over your foot to keep it from going places it shouldn't go. Your foot doesn't have a mind of its own. Your foot doesn't wake up in the morning and say, "I'm going down the street and rob that convenience store." Then you, who are asleep, are suddenly dragged out of bed by this wayward foot and are bounced down the stairs and out the door to the convenience store down the street. You try to stay on your feet as you are pulled down the street. Even though you realize that you are in your night clothes, you can't do anything to get back to your house. You watch as houses pass by you because this foot attached to your body is determined to have its way.

No, of course not. YOU have control over where your feet go. Did you ever sing this song as a child? I don't know who wrote this song but my mother sang this to me as a child. We also sang it in Sunday School.

"Oh, be careful little eyes what you see.
Oh, be careful little eyes what you see.
For the Father up above He is looking down in love
Oh, be careful little eyes what you see."

Then you sing it again and change the word "eyes" to the word "hands." Repeat the song changing the word to "feet" and then repeat it again and change it to "mouth."

From little children, we are taught to watch what we see, do, where we go and what we say. WE ARE RESPONSIBLE for what we observe, what we do, where we go and what we say. God isn't. He has instructed us how to live righteously but then it's up to us whether or not we live that way.

Peer pressure can't get you OUT of trouble but it sure can get you INTO trouble. How do I know? I've been there.

When I was in the fifth grade, the whole grade had a wonderful opportunity to go down to the local theatre and see the movie, "Lassie." It was wonderful for us because this was a small town with maybe one or two traffic lights at the time, and the most excitement we ever had was riding around the town and county on Christmas Eve night to see everyone's Christmas lights before going back home and opening our presents. We opened our presents on Christmas Eve because Mama was preparing Christmas dinner for company on Christmas morning and didn't want to be distracted.

My mother had allowed me to go home with a friend of mine from school, Jana, to spend the night and then go to see the movie the next day with my grade. Mama had bought me a red pair of shorts with two or three shiny brass-colored buttons down the side of the legs for me to play in at Jana's house. The shorts covered my legs to just above my knee. I was never allowed to wear shorts except for playtime. Anywhere else I went, I had to wear a dress. My mother had given me strict instructions that I was not to wear the shorts to school. I knew all the other girls were wearing shorts and I didn't want to be different, but my mother wouldn't hear of me wearing anything but my dress.

When I went home with Jana, she couldn't understand why I couldn't wear shorts to school, especially to see the movie. It was the type of thing to which you wore shorts. After an afternoon of play and talking that night before bed, I decided to disobey my mother and wear those red shorts to the movie. I knew I was disobeying but I did it anyway. I just didn't want to be different and I really couldn't understand why I couldn't wear them. It didn't matter whether or not my mother might be wrong in her thinking; it mattered that I knew I was disobeying her.

The next morning I dressed for school in my red shorts with that knowing disobedience still nagging in the back of my mind. When I got to school, it felt so nice to fit in with the other girls. All of us were dressed casually in shorts. We went to the theatre and sat down in those hard wooden seats, but we didn't care because we were so excited to get out of school to see a movie. I had purchased an orange drink. At some point, either someone bumped me or I was just clumsy, but I spilled that drink all over my nice red shorts. I couldn't get rid of the stain. When I got home that afternoon, I had to explain to my mother why I had this huge stain on my shorts, plus I had to explain why I was even wearing shorts. I don't remember if she punished me or not.

My point is that I chose to disobey because I didn't want to be different and I was encouraged by a peer to disobey. Regardless of what words my friend used to "encourage" me, the choice was still MINE.

The same goes for you in any situation where one or more of your peers are "encouraging" you to participate in something you know is wrong or it is

74

in direct disobedience to something your parents have specifically told you not to do. You have the choice of whether you want to fit in or take a stand and be different.

ဆ ~ ઉઝ

Review Questions for Chapter 4

1. In thinking about peer pressure, what does the title of this chapter mean to you?

2. Can you think of an incident where you had to do what Angie did in the story at the beginning of this chapter?

3. What did Jesus do when the crowd tried to push Him off a cliff?

4. When you are faced with situations involving peer pressure, what choices do you have?

5. According to Proverbs 1:7-9, how does a man become wise? Who refuses to be taught?

6. If God's Word tells you to do or NOT do something, do you have a choice of whether or not to obey?

Chapter 5
Flattering Lips

"O-o-o-h!!! That looks so good on you! You just have to buy it," Fran told Jennifer as Jennifer stood looking at herself in the department store dressing room mirror. "It really shows your figure and it shows that you really DO have a figure."

"You think so?" Jennifer questioned as she stood admiring herself from every angle that the mirrors made available. She was fourteen years old and developing into a very pretty young lady. However, what she was seeing in that mirror was a very skimpily clad young lady. Jennifer had tried on a two-piece bikini bathing suit that showed more skin that she had ever shown in public.

Jennifer's parents had taught her to dress modestly. They had shown her from God's Word about dressing modestly so she knew that wearing that style of bathing suit in public was wrong. Because she was a Christian, her conscience was governed by the Holy Spirit Who had come to dwell inside her spirit man when she accepted Jesus as her Lord and Savior. Her conscience was a God-given gift to her to keep her from doing something she would later regret.

Jennifer stared at herself, turning this way and that and noticing just how skimpy that bathing suit was. "I don't know," she finally said with hesitation in her voice at buying it. "I'm not used to wearing something like this. My mother and father would not approve."

"Listen," Fran said with an air of authority in her voice, "you can only wear it when you and I go to the beach. Your parents will never know. Go ahead and buy it. I'll even keep it at my house for you. In fact, if you want, I'll buy it now and you can pay me back later."

Fran had certainly made it easy for Jennifer. All she had to do was say, "Okay," and the deal was done. Would she do it? If she did allow Fran to buy it for her at the time, would she follow through and violate her conscience by wearing it to the beach?

I'm not going to finish the story since this was just a story, but put yourself in Jennifer's situation. BOYS, I know you don't wear bikinis, but what about skimpy bathing suits designed for boys? The principle is the same in both situations.

Proverbs chapter 7 and verses 21 through 23 give a clue as to what flattery does. Read the verses before this for yourself. I am just going to briefly share the context of those verses. A woman who sells her body was walking down the street and she met a young man. It didn't matter that it happened to be this young man; any young man would have satisfied her. She was looking to practice evil and she didn't care that she was drawing this young man into her evil ways. Upon seeing this young man, she started trying to get him to go with her. She talked and talked and said things that she thought would convince him that it was okay to go with her. The Living Bible states in verses 21 and 22 that

". . .she seduced him with her pretty speech, her coaxing and her wheedling, until he yielded to her. He couldn't resist her flattery. He followed her as an ox going to the butcher, or as a stag that is trapped, waiting to be killed with an arrow through its heart. He was as a bird flying into a snare, not knowing the fate awaiting it there."

Now, look at verse 21 in the Amplified translation.

"With her much justifying and enticing argument she persuades him, with the

allurements of her lips she leads him [to overcome his conscience and his fears] and forces him along."

What was this woman doing? She was using flattery as a manipulative tool to get what SHE wanted. She didn't care what it would do to the other person. She only wanted the satisfaction of knowing that she could "force" this person to do what SHE wanted.

Your Conscience

Before we go any further, what is your conscience? Does everyone have a conscience? Is a conscience worth having? Would you like to try to live without a conscience? Does the Bible talk about us having a conscience?

Proverbs chapter 20 and verse 27 gives a clear definition of what our conscience does.

"A man's conscience is the Lord's searchlight exposing his hidden motives."

In the King James version, it states,

"The spirit of man is the candle of the Lord, searching all the inward parts of the belly."

It is referring to a man's spirit, your spirit man, the inner part of you that becomes born again when you accept Jesus as Lord of your life. Your spirit man and your conscience are meshed. Your conscience talks to you out of your spirit. Think of it as your spirit man being a big pot of what you have stored in there regarding the right way to live and the wrong way according to God's Word. All of us have stored things in our spirit man all our lives. Some things we have stored because we read it directly from God's Word. Other things we have stored because our parents taught us. Your conscience takes a big ladle, dips into that pot, and brings up those things. Then, when you are faced with a situation of whether to do right or wrong, your conscience speaks up inside you and either says, "That's the right thing to do," or "That's the wrong thing to do."

When you become a Christian, your conscience comes alive to what is stored in your spirit man. Your conscience quickens you to things. Have you ever had a piece of hanging fingernail and tried to pull it off and pulled it too far? What happened? Did it feel good? Did you want to holler? Did you holler in pain? If you pulled it too far, then you pulled it down into what we call "the quick." You pulled that piece of fingernail down so far that it got into the part of your finger that was alive to pain. Pain didn't have to tell you that it was there. You felt it. That's what your conscience does. Your conscience doesn't have to tell you that it is there. You feel it, or we could say, sense it inside you. You hear your conscience talking to you. God will use your conscience to talk to you.

According to God's Word in Proverbs 20:27, your conscience is the Lord's searchlight. What is the purpose of a searchlight? Of course, it is to search. What does "to search" mean? You look for something. If someone is lost in the woods at night, people will take a searchlight out in the woods to look for that person. They will shine that light on every piece of ground looking for signs that the person is there or has been there. God's searchlight is looking for something. What might that be? This verse says that God gave you a conscience so your conscience would search out hidden motives, hidden reasons of why you are doing a certain thing or why you aren't doing a certain thing. God doesn't share this with the whole world. Your conscience is inside you to tell YOU, not someone else. Your conscience is your safeguard against rashly doing something. That means doing something without thinking.

That brings us to another point. Can your conscience MAKE you do something or STOP you from doing something? NO!!! WHY? Because God created you with a will. You always have a choice of whether or not you participate in something which your conscience has told you wasn't right to do.

You aren't a robot. No one can program you to do something against your will. No one can turn dials on you or punch keys to MAKE you do something they want. They can influence you by what they say and do which is what this woman in

Proverbs 7:21, 22 did. She used flattery to get this young man to go with her. At any time this young man could have taken her arm and given it back to her and walked away, but he didn't. He listened; he looked; and he thought. The whole time she was painting him a picture, he was meditating on it and he liked what he saw. All that time, his conscience was saying, "Don't look at her. Don't listen to her. What she is suggesting is wrong. Don't go with her." But what did he do? He told his conscience to shut up and went with her.

What did the Amplified translation say about his conscience? This woman led him to **OVERCOME his conscience and his fears.** That means his conscience was speaking to him but **HE CHOSE** to ignore it.

What did the Living Bible say about her using flattery as a tool to capture him? It said that she SEDUCED him with her pretty SPEECH. So, she used words that she knew would tickle his ears. She knew what to say that he wanted to hear. She coaxed and wheedled him. She encouraged him to come to her. In other words, she was applying pressure with her words to get him to make a decision to go her way.

In the end, what happened to this young man? He yielded to her. WHY? He couldn't resist her flattery. Of course, he COULD resist. He didn't want to resist. He allowed himself to become caught up in the excitement of the moment of what he thought he was going to experience and he refused to listen to his conscience. He let this woman do ALL the talking. He just let her talk and let her words go down into his spirit man which silenced his conscience. It was his decision.

That's what will happen to you if you allow it. It's your choice. Always remember that you have a choice to yield or not yield. Don't ever think that you have to yield to peer pressure from anyone. No, you don't. Girls, if you are in a situation where a boy is trying to get you to do something you know is wrong, don't yield. If he is telling you that you are crazy for not doing it or you're a wimp or whatever he is telling you trying to get you to yield to him, don't do it and don't believe him. Listen to your conscience. **Don't allow flattering lips to seduce, coax and wheedle you into doing something you know is wrong.** Any boy who is trying to get you to do something against your conscience is not worth knowing. He just placed himself on your "Not Worth Knowing" list.

Boys, if you are in a situation where a girl is trying to use her body to get your attention or dressing in a way to cause you to look at her in the wrong manner, don't allow her to influence you. Look away and walk away. She's not worth knowing. Put her on your "Not Worth Knowing" list.

Flattering Tongues Trap

People who use flattering tongues to get people to go their way are using their tongues as a trap. Didn't we just see that in Proverbs chapter 7 and verses 21 and 22? Didn't we see that in the beginning story where Jennifer was trying on that bathing suit and her friend was flattering her into wearing it when she knew she shouldn't? Look at this verse

Proverbs 29:5, 6
"Flattery is a trap; evil men are caught in it, but good men stay away and sing for joy."

H-m-m-m, did you catch the last part of that verse? See, when you read God's Word, you have to trust the Holy Spirit within you to help you "catch" things. The Holy Spirit is inside you to bring revelation knowledge to you about God's Word. He is there to show you more about God's Word than what you see right in front of your eyes. He takes you deeper. No man or woman can do that. That is the Holy Spirit's job.

So, what did you catch? Well, you know flattery is a trap. We just talked about that. Those who have their minds directed toward evil are caught in it because they disregard their consciences. Those who have their minds directed toward righteousness, or what God says is right, stay away from flattery. They recognize it immediately

85

and just leave. They don't hang around to listen and allow it to get its hooks in them. Now, we come to the last part. What do those good men do who stay away from flattery? THEY SING FOR JOY. They do what? **THEY SING FOR JOY.** WHY? They walked away from a situation that could steal their joy. Flattery will steal your joy. Since flattery is part of peer pressure, what will peer pressure do? STEAL YOUR JOY. **Anything that purposely steals your joy is not of God.** What does that make flattery? Is it of God? Of course not.

Flattering Tongues and Ulterior Motives

Do people who flatter have what we call "ulterior motives"? Those are motives that bring some kind of reward to the person who is doing the flattering. This person has a hidden reason for doing what he is doing. It may look as if he is doing it for one reason but, in actuality, he is doing it for another reason. You may not know what that reason is.

Let's look at this verse in the Amplified translation.

Proverbs 27:14
"The flatterer who loudly praises and glorifies his neighbor, rising early in the morning, it shall be counted as cursing him [for he will be suspected of sinister purpose]."

Think about this verse for a moment. Think about yourself. Think if every time you went to school, a particular student would come up to you and flatter you with words. They might seem harmless to the ear, but this happens every day. In fact, this person makes a point of coming to you at a particular time in a particular place to flatter you with words and he doesn't do this in secret. He talks very loudly so all those around can hear exactly what he is saying to you. What would you think? I can tell you what I would think. "What is wrong with you? Just what are you up to?" What did Proverbs 27:14 say? Anyone who flatters like that has turned good words into a curse because he will be suspected of being up to something. The person to whom he is speaking the flattering words will think that he is out to harm them in some way. Who wouldn't think that?

Flattery and Hatred

Here is what flattery is according to God's Word.

Proverbs 26:28
"Flattery is a form of hatred and wounds cruelly."

Is God's Word strong or what? Can you take it? Don't run. Plant your feet right where they are and read this. **Whatever God's Word says to you is for your good.** God always works for your good.

God is a good God and always wants good for you so take His Word like medicine and allow it to work good in your life.

Flattery is a form of hatred. How can that be? When a person hates another person what is going on there? The person who is doing the hating does not care about the welfare or health of the other person. They don't care what might be going on in that person's life. They just don't care. Flattery doesn't care about the other person. Flattery only cares about flattery. Isn't that what we said about peer pressure earlier? **Peer pressure only cares about peer pressure.** Peer pressure is self-centered. Instead of flattery bringing healing to a person's life, it wounds. It's a cruel thing to do to someone else.

Psalm chapter 5 and verse 9 says that those who flatter have tongues **". . .filled with flatteries to gain their wicked ends."**

As we saw earlier in Proverbs 27:14, the one who flatters has a purpose in mind. Psalm 5:9 bears this out also. The one who flatters is out to gain something for himself.

What can save a person from flattery? Proverbs 2:16 says that only wisdom from God can. Your earthly wisdom can't do it. How do you get God's wisdom? By reading His Word and practicing what you read. You will become strong in the Lord by staying with Him.

Frankness is Appreciated

Here's a final thought about flattery from Proverbs chapter 28 and verse 23.

"In the end, people appreciate frankness more than flattery."

Flattery may look like it makes the person feel good at the moment, but all it does is hurt the person. They would appreciate you much more if you will just tell the truth. The word "frankness" means to tell the truth. Don't cover it with flattery. Be a REAL person.

Here's an exercise for you. Take the story at the beginning of this chapter and change Fran from being a flatterer to a friend who is being frank.

ജ ~ ᥊

Review Questions for Chapter 5

1. In the beginning story, what was the purpose of Jennifer's conscience?

2. According to Proverbs 20:27, what is a man's conscience?

3. How does God use your conscience?

4. Why can't your conscience make you do something or stop you from doing something?

5. According to Proverbs 29:5, 6, what is flattery?

6. What will peer pressure steal from you?

7. Describe flattery as stated in Proverbs 26:28.

8. According to Proverbs 28:23, what do people appreciate more than flattery?

9. Can you think of an instance where you were flattered but you would have preferred otherwise?

Chapter 6
Gossiping Tongues

"Ow, that hurt!" Have you ever uttered that phrase? Have you ever had a car door slammed on your finger? How about a regular door? How about a drawer of some kind? I have had a file drawer close on my fingers and been in so much pain that I couldn't holler, "Ow, that hurt!" When I was about 11 years old, I experienced the pain of a car door being slammed on my fingers. My mother and I lived on a farm in the country with my grandparents. My grandmother had a friend who lived in town. This friend had a granddaughter about my age, maybe a little younger. My grandmother and I went to town one particular morning and picked up this friend and her granddaughter to come spend the day with us. We all had a wonderful time and when that time was over, my grandmother and I took them back to town and dropped them off at their house. My grandmother's friend was disciplining her granddaughter with her tongue as they were getting out of the car, and she wasn't watching what she was doing. I was trying to get out of the car and had put my hand in the wrong place. It was my fault. The friend slammed the car door while directing her granddaughter into the house, but when she slammed the door, my fingers were directly in its path. My fingers erupted in pain. I started screaming. Someone opened the car door and I retrieved my hurting fingers and just held them. I was probably crying, too. This friend was so upset at having done such a thing that she gave me a quarter. She never would have slammed the door on my fingers on purpose. It was an accident, but the pain was so horrific that the incident has stayed in my mind all these years.

As horrific as that pain was, that is how horrific your words to someone else or about someone else can be. Unless a person knows how to allow someone's words roll off them like water off a duck's back, words can hurt and damage someone. Gossiping tongues, or we could say, gossiping words, can greatly hurt another person. Not only does it hurt the one who is being gossiped about, but it hurts the one doing the gossiping.

What does the word "gossip" mean? Webster's dictionary defines this word as meaning, *"idle talk or rumor, esp. about the personal or private affairs of others."* (2) Some synonyms of that word are *"small talk, hearsay, palaver, chitchat."*

Did you notice the first part of that definition? Idle talk. Did you know that Jesus made mention of "idle talk" in the book of Matthew? He said in Matthew chapter 12 and verse 36 that

". . .you must give account on Judgment Day for every idle word you speak."

Did you see that? What does "give account" mean? If your parents give you a job to do like clean out the garage, what are you expected to do? Of course, you are expected to clean out the garage. How much of the garage are you expected to clean? All of it unless they specify that only a certain part be cleaned. If they say that they will come check on you in about 2 or 3 hours, what are they doing? They are coming to see how much you have done on cleaning out the garage. If you have wasted your time and only have a small section of the garage cleaned because you were "idling your time" away, then you are going to have to "give account" to them as to why you haven't completed more of your task. They know what you are capable of doing which is why they gave you that job. They know that if you are capable of cleaning the whole garage or even most of it, that in 2 or 3 hours, you should have a certain amount done.

The same principle applies to your school work. When your teacher assigns you homework, you are expected to do it. She knows you are capable of doing it and that you are capable of turning it in on time. If she didn't believe that you were capable of that, she wouldn't assign the work. When you are supposed to turn in an assignment the next morning, your teacher will hold you accountable by asking for the assignment. If she didn't hold you accountable, she would just ignore you and the assignment and never ask for it. As a teacher, her job is not just to teach you material, but also to hold you accountable for what she has taught. Part of that accountability is having you do homework and turning in your assignments on time.

In the same manner, God knows what we are capable of concerning the words of our mouths. He also knows that speaking wrong words can hurt ourselves as well as hurt others. When we do not use our words constructively, we are speaking "idle words" and we will be held accountable for speaking those words.

Have you ever gossiped about someone or had someone gossip about you? I'm sure we have all experienced one or the other or maybe both. This is an area in which Christians really need to work. The Bible, in some translations, refers to a gossiper as a talebearer. They mean the same thing. We're going to be looking at some verses on gossiping. **Gossiping tongues are a form of peer pressure.** Gossiping individuals can apply pressure upon those to whom they gossiping to join in their conversation about another individual. They can also apply pressure to those about whom they're gossiping. They can apply pressure to force them to yield to their will or even keep them from being friends with someone or forbid them from visiting a certain place.

Gossipers Spread Rumors

Let's look at what God's Word says about gossip and those who gossip.

Proverbs 11:13
"A gossip goes around spreading rumors, while a trustworthy man tries to quiet them."

What does a gossiper do? He or she goes around spreading rumors. What are "rumors"? Let's go to the dictionary again. According to Webster's dictionary, the word "rumor" means, *"a story or statement in general circulation without confirmation or certainty as to facts; gossip; hearsay." (3)*

Can we say that any simpler? I believe so. Let's try. A rumor is when someone starts telling something that they don't know to be true which they usually heard from someone else who heard it from someone else who heard it..... You get the picture. Most of the time the person spreading the rumor doesn't know whether or not what he is spreading is true. I can give you two examples from my own life.

The first example occurred when I was in the eighth grade. Someone started this ridiculous rumor that on February 14, Valentine's Day, some aliens were going to land and capture all the girls and haul them off to some unknown planet. Would you believe it scared some of us girls? Whoever was spreading that rumor had done such a good job that we were actually believing it. Can you tell that we were VERY impressionable?

The other example happened when I was about 26. I was working in a hardware store in my hometown. God had opened a door for me to move to another state. Don't you think that I was old enough? Yes, I was. However, several people in that town, who apparently didn't have enough to do, started spreading rumors and gossiping. A friend of mine called me and said that a particular young man, whom I knew but was not friends with, had come into the store where she worked and said that he heard that I was leaving to join the Moonies. If you don't know who "the Moonies" were, they were a group of people who were known as a cult. They weren't known as a good group to be with because they didn't serve Jesus Christ as Lord of their lives. Now, I knew that I wasn't going to run off to join some cult, and I knew that I had never said anything like that to anyone. I don't know where that person got his information but his mouth caused quite a stir. Somewhere, someone's mouth started that information which was WRONG information. They didn't have any business starting it and those who heard it didn't have any business spreading it.

God didn't create us to be gossip "carrier pigeons" for Him. If we carry anything for Him, we are to carry the gospel of Jesus Christ to a lost world. If we are actively doing that, we don't have time to run our mouths against anyone.

Now, look at the second part of that verse. While a gossiper goes around SPREADING rumors, what does a trustworthy man do? He is working to quiet them. How can one quiet them? Sometimes, it's just a matter of turning away from the person and leaving him standing there with his rumor. If he doesn't have anyone to tell it to, he can't continue to spread it. Sometimes, you may need to say something like, "It doesn't matter if that is true or not, God didn't create my ears to be garbage cans. I don't want to hear it and I refuse to listen." Then, walk away from them.

The Urge to Gossip

Why does a gossiper continue to gossip? Look at this next verse.

Proverbs 18:8
"What dainty morsels rumors are. They are eaten with great relish!"

Now, let's look at this same verse in the Amplified translation of the Bible.

"The words of a whisperer or talebearer are as dainty morsels; they go down into the innermost parts of the body."

What do you think that means? What does a "dainty morsel" mean to you? Think of some delicious candy or some delicious dessert. When my husband and I ate at a particular restaurant, they had a dessert called Chocolate Raspberry cake. It looked delicious and so we got a piece and split it. It was very good. To us, that was a dainty morsel. That piece of cake was so good to us and satisfied a part of us that wanted something sweet.

When a person spreads rumors and finds someone who loves to hear rumors, the effect on both of them is as if they had eaten a piece of delicious cake or some other delicious dessert. It satisfies something inside them that craves that sensation. They love it so much that they will go out and try to find someone else to share that rumor with so they will enjoy that delicious sensation all over again. It's like being on a drug high for them. They never get enough and are always looking for another way to "get high" again.

Don't Trust a Blabbermouth

Should you tell someone a secret whom you know to be a gossip? Do I need to answer that for you? God's Word does it for me.

Proverbs 20:19
"Don't tell your secrets to a gossip unless you want them broadcast to the world."

Isn't the Bible plain? What's another word for someone who can't keep a secret? I can think of one—blabbermouth. If you know someone cannot keep a secret, don't tell them anything. I have had friends over the years that I trusted to keep secrets and then found out later that they didn't. You probably have, too.

Gossip Causes Tension

What does gossip cause? The Bible states that gossip causes tension.

Proverbs 26:20
"Fire goes out for lack of fuel, and tensions disappear when gossip stops."

Did you know that gossip can split up friendships? Did you know that gossip can cause splits between people in your church? Did you know that gossip can taint someone's influence in a particular area? Another way to use the word "taint" in this sentence would be to say that gossip can hurt someone's influence. It can make him ineffective.

Let's say that you have a wonderful teacher, but he *[I am using the pronoun "he" but you know it could be a "she."]* is considered by many to be a hard teacher. "Hard" doesn't mean that the teacher is harsh. It means that the teacher has high standards for his students and expects his students to strive to meet those high standards. When this teacher assigns homework, he expects every student to do it. Starting the homework and not finishing it is not doing it. When I taught school, I had a few students who started on their homework right after school while they were waiting for their parents to pick them up or while they were in the aftercare program, but that was all they did. The next morning they turned in an incomplete paper and it was consistently that way.

Let's go back to our "hard" teacher. As this teacher expects you to complete your work and do your best in his class, it is putting a good form of pressure on you to come up higher. However, your flesh just doesn't want to do that. Your flesh has become used to being lazy and doing what IT wants instead of what it has been told to do. You just don't want to exercise any authority over your flesh to get up and do your homework like you should. So, what might you do? I said "might" because I know you would NEVER do this.

You start grumbling and complaining. To whom? Well, at first it's to your fellow classmates. *[All the names I am using here are fictitious.]* "That Mr. Farris is just too hard. He's being mean to us. He's giving us way too much homework and on a weekend, too. Who does he think he is to give us so much work? I hope he gets fired."

If you find some willing classmates who will listen, then they will pick up the gossip. That's what it is—gossip. "Yeah, this homework thing is a bummer. I've got soccer practice after school and how does he expect me to do my homework and practice, too. Maybe he will get fired."

Once, this gets started through the classroom and has been fueled by mouth after mouth, the students take it into their individual homes. "Mom, Mr. Farris is just giving us too much homework. I don't think he understands that we can't do all that and keep up our sports, too."

Mom, who loves her child greatly and can't stand the thought of anyone hurting her dear one, takes up the discourse. "How much homework is he giving you?" she asks her "innocent" child.

Realizing that he has captured his mother's attention, he jumps right in, "Look. We've got this in history, this in math, and this in English. That's not counting my other subjects. He's so unfair."

His mother immediately sides with her child without praying about the situation or even going to Mr. Farris and talking with him. She goes to the phone and calls a mother of one of the other students. "Beverly, is your child having problems in Mr. Farris' class?"

"Well," Beverly said, "now that you mention it. Julia just came home today complaining about so much homework. She said all the kids in class were complaining."

This conversation is the fuel for the gossip tree. As one person talks to another, the rumors spread until the whole school has heard about how unfair Mr. Farris is and how he is overworking his students.

Now, what these dear parents and students have not taken the time to find out is that Mr. Farris was sent to that school by God to bring those students up to a higher level academically and spiritually. He was not sent there to pamper them and allow them to get away with sloppiness and laziness. He was sent there to hold them accountable. He truly cared about each and every student and only wanted the best for them.

However, the gossiping worsened. So, what happens to Mr. Farris' influence at that school? It drops to the point that Mr. Farris has to leave. He doesn't want to leave. He hasn't done anything wrong that he would need to leave, but people's gossiping mouths have so hurt his influence that the parents don't trust him and the students don't have any respect for him. There isn't anything he can do but leave.

Was that right? No. What he did was right but what the parents and students did by gossiping wasn't. God will hold THEM accountable for their actions.

The Power of the Tongue

Here's a verse that talks about the power of the tongue.

Proverbs 18:21 (Amplified translation)
"Death and life are in the power of the tongue, and they who indulge it shall eat the fruit of it [for death or life]."

With your tongue, you can speak life over a person or yourself or you can speak death over another person or yourself. Whatever you allow your tongue to speak, you will eat the fruit of those words. **Your words do bear fruit.** You can't stop them from bearing. To indulge your tongue means that you allow your tongue to say anything it wants, anytime it wants, and never consider the consequences of what you are saying. Here are some examples:

- Blurting things out without thinking first

- Giving someone a "piece of your mind"
- Joining into a conversation of gossip about someone else
- Looking for an opportunity to gossip
- Hunting someone up just to talk about someone else

Gossip is a Form of Strife

Proverbs 16:28
"An evil man sows strife; gossip separates the best of friends."

Did you see that? A gossiper and an evil man are in the same verse. Do you think they might be considered the same? **Strife is a separator.** Two people cannot be in strife and agree, and two people cannot walk together unless they are in agreement. Gossip is one of those things that separates good friends. Actually, whoever is listening to the gossip should know better than to listen to anything about their good friend. God considers gossip to be evil and those who practice it are practicing evil.

Idle Words

Look at this verse.

Proverbs 16:27
"Idle hands are the devil's workshop; idle lips are his mouthpiece."

God doesn't speak idle words so when you or I allow our lips to utter idle words, who are we allowing to influence us? If it's not God, then it's _____. You know. I don't have to tell you.

God Looks at Motives

Whatever words we speak, our motives are involved.

Proverbs 21:2
"We can justify our every deed but God looks at our motives."

WOW!!! How does God see our motives? He looks at our hearts. Did you know that? You should. God doesn't look at what you do on the outside. He is intently looking at your heart ALL the time because whatever is in your heart is what you will do through your flesh.

Let's go back to our example of Mr. Farris. If we were to put that first student who started the gossip about Mr. Farris on trial and asked him, "Andrew, why did you start talking about Mr. Farris?" what would he do? He would try to justify why he did that. He might say, "I started talking about Mr. Farris because what he was doing was unfair." That is what all the people in the courtroom would hear and use to judge the situation, BUT God had another yardstick to use to measure Andrew's justification. God goes straight to Andrew's heart and this is what Andrew's heart is saying, "I hate homework and I don't like Mr. Farris. I don't want him as my teacher so I'm going to see if I can get others to agree with me and maybe we'll run him off. I would love to see him get fired."

Now, let's take this to the parents who got involved in this gossiping. Andrew's mother was the first one to begin gossiping in the parent arena. If we were to put her on trial and asked her, "Mrs. Newport, why did you start talking about Mr. Farris?" what would she do? She would try to justify why she started gossiping about him. "My child's life was at stake here. I didn't want that man ruining his opportunity to become a good student and graduating when he should. He was preventing my child from participating in sports like he wanted and I don't think that is right." Again, her response is what those in the courtroom would hear. What would God see and hear? He would look at her heart and her motives for doing what she did. This what HE hears coming from her heart, "That man is making life hard for me. It was so easy raising Andrew and not having to stand over him to make him do his homework because he didn't have much homework. Now, this man comes into his life and demands more from him and me. I don't want to do it. I've got too many other things that I want to do and my child's education is not my number one priority. I have a life, too, and I'm not going to allow this man to change my lifestyle. It thrills me to think that he might get fired and get kicked out of this school."

Does that take your breath away? God can peel back the covers and see what's underneath. Nothing is hidden from Him.

You Control Your Tongue

Do you have control over your tongue? Can you control what you say? Remember, we have said before that if God's Word says that you are to do something, then that means you have the power and the choice to do it. So, let's go to God's Word.

Proverbs 10:14
"A wise man holds his tongue. Only a fool blurts out everything he knows; that only leads to sorrow and trouble."

Who "holds his tongue"? A fool? Is that what God's Word said? No, of course it didn't. **The person who holds his tongue is a WISE man.**

Now, what did that verse just tell you about God's Word? It is possible for a human being, male or female, to hold his tongue. God lays a choice before each person. You can be like the wise man and do this or you can be like the fool and do this. We always want to aim for wisdom. So, naturally, we want to be like the wise man and hold our tongues.

The second part of that verse describes what a fool will do with information. He shares everything he knows because he wants to talk and likes to hear himself talk. Sometimes, people like that want to share because they like to see how someone is going to react to what they have to say. Just as we discussed earlier about the gossiper who likes to gossip because it is like eating a delicious dessert, a fool likes to blurt out things because it satisfies a hunger in him.

If a person knows something, why isn't it okay for him to share it? Wisdom says that just because you know something about someone or a situation, doesn't mean you are to say anything about it to anyone. As Proverbs chapter 10 and verse 14 stated, it can lead to sorrow and trouble. You can cause hurt feelings between people because you couldn't keep your mouth shut. Some of you need to learn the "S" word. When I taught at a Christian school, I heard one of the parents talking about her daughter who was in the 6th grade at the time. She said she had come home telling her that her coach had used the "S" word that day. At first, her mother thought she meant a dirty word, but the word to which she was referring was the phrase "Shut up." I guess he had become extremely exasperated with them that day. You may not always have someone around you who will tell you to "shut up" so you have to tell yourself.

How do you know when to speak and when not? If you are a Christian, you are going to have to depend upon the Holy Spirit Who dwells inside you. Learn to listen for His voice. As you practice listening for Him about different situations, you will learn to recognize His "Uh-uh's" when you're about to share something with someone you shouldn't or His "That's okay," when you need to share something with someone. There are times when a person needs to know something that you know, but be sensitive to the Spirit of God within you and don't be a blabbermouth or become known as a person who can't stop talking.

Here's a good admonition from God's Word.

Proverbs 21:23
"Keep your mouth closed and you'll stay out of trouble."

Here's another verse about how hurtful your words can be, especially when they are not truthful words.

Proverbs 25:18
"Telling lies about someone is as harmful as hitting him with an axe, or wounding him with a sword, or shooting him with a sharp arrow."

You would not go up to someone and hit him or her with an axe, would you? Criminals do that and you aren't a criminal. Neither would you go up to someone and stick him or her with a sword or we could say shoot a gun at them, would you? No, lawbreakers do that and you are not a lawbreaker. Would you stand at a distance with a bow and arrow, take careful aim, then let the arrow fly free right toward a person? No, again, that is against God's law and the law of the land. What would be the intention in all of these cases? To INTENTIONALLY hurt someone. God's Word says that when you tell a lie about someone, you are INTENTIONALLY hurting him as if you had tried to hit him with an axe, wound him with a sword, or shoot him with an arrow. Don't think you can get past that by saying, "Oh, I was just kidding! Can't you tell when I'm kidding?" No, once you spout a lie about someone, the damage has been done. You can't take back words that have been uttered in the presence of others. Their ears have heard it and most likely at some point, they will repeat what they have heard to someone else.

The best thing to do as we said before is obey God's Word. Here are some more verses.

Proverbs 10:19
"Don't talk so much. You keep putting your foot in your mouth. Be sensible and turn off the flow!"

Proverbs 11:12
". . .a man with good sense holds his tongue."

What's wrong with having a quick tongue? What's wrong with being able to spout something right back to someone? What's wrong with giving back as good as one has been given? This next verse says don't do it.

Proverbs 13:3
"Self-control means controlling the tongue! A quick retort can ruin everything."

I have to admit that there are times when I have seen someone spout something back to someone and it silenced the situation. I witnessed that in a 3rd grade class that I taught. I don't remember what was said at that particular time, but I do remember that one of the boys in the class smarted off to one of the girl students who was having a hard time reading. Before I could say anything to the boy about his behavior, the girl spouted a remark right back to him that silenced him. I stood in amazement. I looked at the boy and said, "_____, she's right."

What occurred in my classroom may not always be the right thing for someone to do. In this case, it was right. This girl was not one who talked a lot or gossiped or was known as a blabbermouth. I had watched her the whole year and she was not that type. I believe that God gave her the right retort to deliver back to her fellow student. The point of Proverbs chapter 13 and verse 3 is that you are not to be known as a person who has absolutely NO control over his tongue to the point that EVERY TIME someone says something to you, you have to "pop off" with a smart remark. If you're that kind of person, then you aren't listening. You will become known as a "smart mouth" and people will not want to have anything to do with you.

There are many more verses I could quote here about truth, lies, and the tongue, but you need to read the whole book of Proverbs yourself and underline or highlight in your Bible every time you see anything about these subjects. Read over them many times and allow the Holy Spirit to bring revelation to you about these topics. That is His job. Let Him do His job in your life. Allow Him to grow you up in Christ Jesus to the place where you can take your place in Christ's body and fill that place the way God created you to fill it. **Become known as a person who doesn't gossip and who is trustworthy.** Don't allow the devil to use you as a gossip to apply pressure to others. Resist him. God has given you the power to resist the devil through the name of Jesus. Use Jesus' name and resist the devil.

Here's a great thought with which to end this chapter. A minister asked God one time this question. "God, how can I most hurt the devil?" He thought God would give him this gigantic revelation of some BIG thing he could do to hurt Satan.

Here is what God said. Are you ready for this? "Don't do what he says."

Do you know that every time you refuse to bow your knee to Satan by not doing what he says, such as refusing to gossip about someone, that you are HURTING him? Make the decision today that every time you hear the enemy tell you to do something that you know is against God's Word that you aren't going to do it. **Don't hurt God; hurt Satan.** Obey God. When you obey God, you are disobeying the enemy's commands and you are causing discomfort and torture to Satan's camp. That's what you WANT to do. Satan should never get a moment's peace around you because you are continually obeying God. Even if you make a mistake, you ask forgiveness, get right back up, and get right back on track. Whatever good time Satan thinks he is about to have won't last because you won't allow him to have that good time. When you open your eyes in the morning, Satan's first reaction to you should be absolute terror, "OH NO!!! HE'S AWAKE!!!"

ℬ ~ ℭ

Review Questions for Chapter 6

1. Define what gossip means to you.

2. Give the Scripture reference in which Jesus warned about our having to give account of every idle word we speak.

3. Have your parents ever held you accountable for something? If so, what?

4. How can gossiping tongues be a form of peer pressure? Have you ever experienced a situation such as that? If so, can you describe it?

5. Proverbs 11:13 contrasts a gossiper with a trustworthy man. Explain the contrast.

6. Make up a story using Proverbs 11:13 as a basis.

7. Explain what Proverbs 26:20 means to you.

8. According to Proverbs 18:21, what two things are in the power of your tongue?

9. Are strife and gossip ever good things? Why or why not?

10. What does Proverbs 21:2 say about our deeds and our motives?

11.   Give three Scripture references in this chapter from Proverbs about keeping your mouth closed. Beside each reference, list the benefits of keeping your mouth closed.

12.   What is your opinion of gossip? Do you believe it helps or hurts people?

Chapter 7
Set Yourself Apart for God's Use

What does the phrase "set yourself apart for God's use" mean? That means that you CONSECRATE yourself to God. No, I didn't say "concentrate." I said "consecrate." The spelling is different. Take note of that. Let me tell you about my grandmother's chair as a way of helping you to see about consecrating something.

My mother was an only child. She did have a brother but he died as a baby. When my mother married at an early age, she and my father lived in the house with her mother and father, my grandparents. My father died when I was nine years old and after my sister married and moved out, that left my grandparents, my mother and myself living in that house.

My grandmother was a tall heftily built woman. At one time she weighed over 200 pounds. Rheumatism in her knees made walking difficult. This affliction also made it hard for her to get up out of certain chairs. In our den, there was one chair that was designated as "Grandma's chair." That was the chair that she always sat in because she could more easily arise from it than from any of the other chairs.

Everyone who knew my grandmother knew that she sat in that chair and if they came to visit, they were warned not to sit in that chair because she had to sit in it. You could say that that chair was "consecrated" for my grandmother's use. Back in the days when salesmen would come door-to-door selling coffee, tea or household items, a salesman came one day and sat in Grandma's chair before we could tell him not to sit there. We heard Grandma lumbering down the hallway, coming toward the den, and decided to wait and see what she would say. She politely asked him to get up and explained that that particular chair was the only one from which she could easily arise. He understood and sat somewhere else.

Consecration simply means being set apart for a special use. That green high-backed chair in our den was "set apart" for our Grandmother's use. She used it so much that it became known as "Grandma's chair." **When you become a Christian you are set apart for a special use.** That special use is whatever God has for you to do.

Now, your will is involved here. As the title stated, there is an understood "YOU" there. YOU set yourself apart for God's use. YOU consecrate yourself to God.

Here is a good definition of how consecration is demonstrated in your life. Paul wrote a letter to the church at Colossae in which he told them how he was praying for them. He prayed for them to be filled with the knowledge of God's will for them and for them to understand spiritual things. One of the reasons he was praying this way for them was explained in verse 10 of chapter 1 in the book of Colossians which is consecration. I am quoting from the Amplified translation.

"That you may walk (live and conduct yourselves) in a manner worthy of the Lord, fully pleasing to Him and desiring to please Him in all things, bearing fruit in every good work and steadily growing and increasing in (and by) the knowledge of God—with fuller, deeper and clearer insight, acquaintance and recognition."

Let's list the points in this verse.

- **Live and conduct yourself in a manner worthy of the Lord**
- **Fully please Him and desire to please Him in all things**
- **Bear fruit in every good work**

- **Steadily grow and increase in and by the knowledge of God**

If you are going to conduct yourself in a manner worthy of the Lord, that means you aren't going to do anything that you know will hurt Him and hurt your testimony as a Christian. As a Christian on this earth, you represent Jesus Christ and when people see you, they should see Jesus because you represent Him. If you do that, then you will fully please Him and you will desire to please Him in all things. Did you catch that? ALL!!! Not one or two, but ALL. That means in every area of your life you desire to please God. If you desire to please God, then you will bear fruit and you will continue to grow in the knowledge of God so that you will readily recognize what God likes and what He doesn't like. You will become well acquainted with Him and His ways. You'll not just know ABOUT God, but you will KNOW Him because you will have spent time with Him in His Word and in prayer.

Let's go to another book that Paul wrote in the New Testament, the book of I Thessalonians. Here Paul is writing a letter to the church in Thessalonica. When I say that he is writing to a church, I mean he is writing to a group of people in Thessalonica who have accepted Jesus as Lord of their lives and who are determining to walk as Christians upon this earth. They are part of the Body of Christ who happen to live in Thessalonica.

Here is what Paul wrote them in chapter 4 starting with verse 1 and going through verse 7. See if you can pick out specific things Paul told them about living a consecrated lifestyle. Again, this is from the Amplified translation.

"Furthermore, brethren, we beg and admonish you in [virtue of our union with] the Lord Jesus, that [you follow the instructions which] you learned from us about how you ought to walk so as to please and gratify God, as indeed you are doing; that you do so even more and more abundantly—attaining yet greater perfection in living this life.

For you know what charges and precepts we gave you [on the authority and by the inspiration of] the Lord Jesus,

For this is the will of God, that you should be consecrated—separated and set apart for pure and holy living: that you should abstain and shrink from all sexual vice;

That each one of you should know how to possess [control, manage] his own body (in purity, separated from things profane, and) in consecration and honor,

Not [to be used] in the passion of lust, like the heathen who are ignorant of the true God and have no knowledge of His will,

That no man transgress, and overreach his brother and defraud him in this matter or defraud his brother in business. For the Lord is an avenger in all these things, as we have already warned you solemnly and told you plainly.

For God has not called us to impurity, but to consecration [to dedicate ourselves to the most thorough purity]."

Did you notice that Paul said, "For this is the will of God..." and proceeded to tell them what the will of God for them was. Now, he wasn't telling them specifically what the will of God for each one of them was down to the minutest detail. Each person has to go to God for himself and find out from God what that is. What he was telling them was about consecrating themselves to God and what that consecration involved. If they refused to consecrate themselves to God and walk worthy of the Lord in those things listed there, they wouldn't even get to know what God had for each one of them to do. **Consecrating yourself to God puts you in a position to receive from God.** That includes blessings from His hand as well as hearing Him speak to you.

Do you think that peer pressure wants you to consecrate yourself to God? After all we've talked about peer pressure and what we just read, what do you REALLY think? The answer is NO. **Peer pressure does not want you to consecrate**

yourself to God; however, peer pressure does want you to consecrate yourself to it. To whatever you consecrate yourself or to whomever you consecrate yourself is the thing or person who is in control of you, or we could say, the thing or person to whom you have given your allegiance. You have pledged to honor that person or that thing. You have given that person or that thing first place in your heart. When you start to do or think anything, that person or that thing will pop up in your mind and heart and be there as a plumb line for your determining what you will do about what you have thought or planned to do.

Here are some things for you to think about concerning every day situations. I'm sure you can add to the list because of things you have experienced or know is happening around you. Don't limit your thinking to just what I have listed. Allow the Holy Spirit to expand the list for you. My list is just to get you STARTED to thinking.

Peer Pressure vs. Consecration

Peer pressure says, "Look at that pair of jeans. That's perfect for you. Everyone is wearing them and you'll just be like one of the crowd. Go on. Buy them. Don't look at how they're made. Your ONLY concern is that you fit in with everyone else. Think of the rush you'll feel when you walk into the room and everyone sees what you're wearing."

Consecration says, "You don't wear something just because it is the fashion of the day. You were created for God's use and you weren't created to fit in with what everyone else is wearing."

ℬ~ℭ

Peer pressure says, "Have a cigarette. See, everyone else is smoking. At least hold it in between your fingers so you'll look as if you're smoking. Okay, you don't have to puff. Just hold it. Come on. Look like everyone else at least. Don't let them know you don't smoke. And hey, take a sip of beer. You don't have to drink the whole bottle. Just hold it and put it up to your lips every now and then and take a small sip. Don't let them know you don't drink. Just look like you're drinking."

Consecration says, "You don't smoke something or drink something nor act as if you are smoking or drinking something just because everyone else is doing it. You weren't created to fit in with what everyone else is drinking or smoking."

ℬ~ℭ

Peer pressure says, "Here comes that bottle. Take a quick sniff. You don't have to stick your nostrils in it. Just pass it under your nose as if

you're sniffing. You don't want to let anyone else know that you're not sniffing. That is so uncool. Oh, here comes the bowl of pills. Come on, dip your hand in and take a few. Okay, so you don't want to take them. Just act as if you're taking them. Put your hand up to your mouth, pretend you're popping them in and then swallow as if you are taking them. Don't make the others uncomfortable by not participating."

Consecration says, "You don't sniff something or swallow something nor act as if you are sniffing or swallowing something just because everyone else is doing it. You weren't created to fit in with what everyone else is sniffing or swallowing."

ಹಿ ~ ಏ

Peer pressure says, "It's okay to 'make out' with your girlfriend (or boyfriend). It won't lead to anything. Go ahead. Let your emotions run wild. They're not going to lead you anywhere dangerous. So what if they do. Who's going to know? You don't care. This isn't about anyone but you and your girlfriend (or boyfriend). It's nobody else's business."

Consecration says, "You don't allow your body to be used for ungodly activities just because everyone else is doing it. Your body is the temple of the Holy Ghost and you were not created to allow your emotions to rule you. You take control over your emotions and don't allow your body to be placed into a situation where your emotions could get out of control."

ℰ ~ ℭ

Peer pressure says, "Haven't you noticed that you're a gay (or lesbian)? Haven't you heard those other teens who have been talking about being gay (or lesbian)? Don't you realize that you're like them? Go ahead. Admit that you're gay (or lesbian). It's okay. You'll feel so much better. You'll fit in with them."

Consecration says, "God created you as a male (or female). He did not create an in-between sex. Whatever you were born as, that's what you are. Don't allow anything deter you from what God created you to be."

ℰ ~ ℭ

Peer pressure says, "A great movie is playing over at the theatre. The language uses all kinds of four letter words. Several scenes have nudity in them. The violence is awesome. It's R-rated but you can get someone to help you get in. You have to go so you can tell the others in your group that you went. You don't want to disappoint them. Do you really want to make

them feel bad because you didn't go see it? Make it unanimous. GO!!!"

Consecration says, "You don't allow your eyes to view movies, television or acts of any kind to go contrary to God's Word. You don't allow your feet to travel into places where those acts are happening. You don't allow your ears to hear things that pollute the Word of God in your life. You weren't created to see filth, hear filth or go where filth is being produced. Filth produces filth."

ဢ ~ os

Peer pressure says, "Speak that ugly word. Go ahead. Just say it once and the next time it will be easier. Go ahead. What are you waiting for? SPEAK!!! See, wasn't that easy? The next time you're with your gang of friends, you'll be able to join right in with them. Watch them glow as you say a four-letter ungodly word every other sentence. Practice at home. Don't just limit it to speaking it with your friends. Speak it out in public. Shock people with your language. It's in the movies all the time. What's wrong with it? Nothing. So, go ahead and curse to your heart's content. You don't have to control your tongue and remember, you DO want to fit in."

Consecration says, "You don't allow a froward mouth to operate. You are in control of your mouth. Your mouth does not tell you what to say. You tell it. You only speak words that will enhance the ears of the listener. You do not curse because cursing brings the curse into your life. God is not the damner of things; Satan is. When you use a phrase such as, 'God d____ something,' you are accusing God as being the damner. Your words bring life or death into your life. You weren't created to speak ungodly words just so you would fit in. Your words can separate you from the death of Satan to the life of God or they can separate you from the life of God to the death of Satan."

ᏏᎤ ~ ᏟᎤ

As I said, you can add to this list. In fact, why don't you do that? Think of different activities or situations and think what peer pressure would say, and then, on the other hand, what would consecration say. The bottom line in consecration is asking yourself this question:

DOES THIS PLEASE GOD OR WILL THIS OFFEND HIM?

I want to end this chapter with a song entitled "I Surrender All." This is an old song but a good one of consecration. We used to sing it in our church a lot when I was a child and as a young

128

adult. Of course, I can't sing it to you but I can list the words to a few verses and the chorus.

I Surrender All
Words by: Judson W. Van DeVenter (1896)
Music by: Winfield S. Weeden (1896)

Verse 1
All to Jesus, I surrender;
All to Him I freely give;
I will ever love and trust Him,
In His presence daily live.

Chorus
I surrender all,
I surrender all,
All to Thee, my blessed Savior,
I surrender all.

Verse 2
All to Jesus I surrender;
Humbly at His feet I bow,
Worldly pleasures all forsaken;
Take me, Jesus, take me now.

ઠ ~ 03

Review Questions for Chapter 7

1. Explain what consecration means to you.

2. If you want to please God, how will you conduct yourself or behave everyday?

3. What does consecrating yourself to God put you in a position to do?

4. What is peer pressure's view of consecration?

5. If you are truly desirous to please God and set yourself apart for HIS use, what question can you ask yourself that will help you determine whether what you are doing or about to do is right or wrong?

Chapter 8
God Loves You

I cannot end this book without emphatically telling you that GOD LOVES YOU. What I have shared with you may seem harsh. Please do not receive it that way. Everything I have shared I have prayed over and attempted to obtain the mind of Christ concerning every chapter.

One of the things I appreciate about God's character is His truth. I never have to be concerned that God is lying to me.

Hebrews 6:18
". . .for it is impossible for God to tell a lie. . . ."

There isn't one iota of **untruth** in Him. HE IS ABSOLUTE TRUTH. Whatever God says in His Word that I can have, I can have. Whatever YOU see in God's Word that you can have, you can have. God never lied one time and never will.

Another thing I appreciate about God's character is His unchangeability.

Malachi 3:6
"For I am the Lord—I do not change . . . ."

My Heavenly Father and your Heavenly Father is not a chameleon. He doesn't change in this situation or that situation to be something that His Word says He isn't. Whatever the Word of God says He is, that is what He is. I never have to be concerned that when I go to Him in prayer that He is going to be in a foul mood or an egotistical mood or a lightning-strike mood. He is always the same—kind, gracious, and full of compassion.

God is my Heavenly Father and, in functioning in that role in my life, He has planned for me. He has an expected end for me.

Jeremiah 29:11
"For I know the plans I have for you, says the Lord. They are plans for good and not for evil, to give you a future and a hope."

Take the two characteristics that I just listed above about God and apply them to this verse. God says that He has plans for you. Let's put Him to the test.

- **Did He lie when He said He had plans for you?**
- **If He does have plans for you, will He change His mind about those plans?**

He said that He had good plans for you. Test Him again.

- **Did He lie about saying those plans were good for you?**
- **At some point in your life, will He decide to change those good plans to ones for evil?**

Those plans as described in Jeremiah 29:11 are to give you a future and a hope. It's a goal for you to head toward to fulfill your destiny in this life. Let's test God one more time.

- **Did He lie when He said those plans were to give you a future and a hope? Does He care about your future?**
- **Will He lead you a few steps in those plans and then decide that He just doesn't want to mess with you and abandon you by the wayside?**

If you don't know the answers to these questions, just go back to what we said earlier. God doesn't lie and He doesn't change.

Whatever God has called you to do, that is what He expects you to do.

Romans 11:29
"For God's gifts and his call can never be withdrawn; he will never go back on his promises."

You have a definite calling in this life and no matter what you decide to do with it, **the calling never changes for you.** That's why it is vitally important that you begin at an early age to seek God for His perfect will to be done in your life. Seek Him about whom you are to marry. Seek Him about where you are to attend college. Seek Him about the job you are to have. God is NOT speechless. He will talk to you and He has equipped you with the ability to hear His voice inside you. Trust Him. Ask Him to speak to you about your life and be willing to do what He says. He isn't going to tell you something to do that is going to be contrary to your parents' authority as long as you are under their authority. If your parents are serving God to the best of their ability, God and your parents will work together to help you get on the right pathway. Ask God to speak to them about you. He loves them just as much as He loves you.

I pray that this book has helped you see the danger of yielding to peer pressure. Determine today that you will stand tall as the young man or young woman that God has created you to be. You can do it with His help. You are the apple of His eye.

ဆာ ~ ဗ

Review Questions for Chapter 8

1. Can God lie? Give the Scripture reference to support your answer.

2. Can God change? Give the Scripture reference to support your answer.

3. According to Jeremiah 29:11, describe the plans God has for you.

4. Why is it so important for you to seek God for HIS perfect will for your life?

Endnotes

1. WEBSTER'S ENCYCLOPEDIC UNABRIDGED DICTIONARY OF THE ENGLISH LANGUAGE (New York: Portland House, 1989), p. 1139.
2. Ibid., p. 611.
3. Ibid., p. 1252.

Author Contact Information

To contact the author or for more information on other books by Carolyn B. Anderson, you may do one of the following:

Call toll free: **(866) 942-0790**
Website address: **www.andersonpub.com**

CPSIA information can be obtained at www.ICGtesting.com
Printed in the USA
BVOW011519250313

316399BV00008B/386/A

9 781598 245479